THE LEAST LIKELY

The author would welcome well corroborated information about least likely Christians around the world and throughout history, who have not been included in this first volume.
He can be contacted on desmond.writer@wanadoo.fr.

the
least likely

If God can use them, he can use you!

KEVIN DESMOND

MONARCH
BOOKS

Oxford, UK, & Grand Rapids, Michigan

First published in the UK 2004 by Monarch Books,
(a publishing imprint of Lion Hudson plc),
Mayfield House, 256 Banbury Road, Oxford OX2 7DH.
Tel: +44 (0) 1865 302750 Fax: +44 (0) 1865 302757
Email: monarch@lionhudson.com
www.lionhudson.com

UK ISBN 1 85424 643 7
US ISBN 0 8254 6061 1

Distributed by:
UK: Marston Book Services Ltd, PO Box 269,
Abingdon, Oxon OX14 4YN;
USA: Kregel Publications, PO Box 2607,
Grand Rapids, Michigan 49501.

British Library Cataloguing Data
A catalogue record for this book is available
from the British Library.

*Front cover photo of Joni
used with permission of Joni and Friends*

Book design and production for the publishers by
Bookprint Creative Services
PO Box 827, BN21 3YJ, England.
Printed in Great Britain.

CONTENTS

5

THE LEAST LIKELY: MY OWN STORY

As the compiler of this book, I too am a "least likely".

Although I had been given an Anglican education, after a disturbing experience with a gay chaplain, from 17 to 27 years old, I became more interested in psychic phenomena and clairvoyance. As a journalist specialising in books and articles on the esoteric history of powerboat racing, in 1980 I was invited out to Detroit, the "Motor City", to research the biography of a millionaire playboy powerboat racing champion of the 1920s called Gar Wood.

The man who welcomed me into his house and home, Harold C Mistele, was chairman of the board of a company which had, for over half a century, been supplying oil and coal to such insatiable auto giants as Ford and General Motors.

Imagine my surprise on discovering that Harold Mistele, his wife and the employees of his business were all devout Christians. At first I felt acutely embarrassed each time they prayed. But the day before I left Detroit, the wife of Harold's pastor asked me a question which was to change my life:

"You die and you meet our Lord Jesus. He asks you, 'When you were on earth, how did you stand up for me?' What would you reply?"

This turning point on my personal road back to the love of Jesus Christ had taken place in the least likely of situations. It also sowed the seed which would eventually flower into this book . . .

INTRODUCTION

This book will take you on a journey of discovery of the most simple but awe-inspiring aspect of life: the way God works. Once you understand the divine strategy, things become clearer . . .

It was made clear to me in only a matter of days. Leading up to this, my own Christian life had been at a low ebb. Admittedly, I was 52 years old and had spent much of my life questioning. Yet the formulation of an initial five-page essay took very little time, even though I am neither an ordained priest nor a professor of theology.

Indeed, the more good people I was led to discover and research for this book, the more I realised my own poverty and unfaithfulness as a Christian. My behaviour was often far from the teachings of our Lord Jesus and Saint Paul. I had lost count of the communions I had participated in and the sermons I had listened to. I was the prodigal son who alternated between his father's house and elsewhere. While God chose to use my talents as a writer and researcher to make a book about his way, I was still a seed which had fallen among thorns. But then one day I heard an inner voice tell me "That is precisely why I have chosen you for this task."

This is only a selection. You can also make cluster groups for further study on such topics as atheists, women, children, soldiers, for example.

My thanks go to the following friends: Carlo Galluzzo, Marc Stefanini, Chris Fairnington, David Gerrish, Fran Tattersall, Louis Requième, André Joubert, Daphne Regan, Michael Selman, and others who have suggested the least likely candidates. Also, I am deeply indebted to so many well prepared websites found using Internet search engines.

Kevin Desmond, Bordeaux, France, January 2004

1. The human and the divine

Consider for a moment. There is a strange difference between the human and the divine way of doing things.

Whenever determined humans plan a challenging mission, they naturally try to reduce the obstacles to a minimum. Such missions can range from sending a space probe into a distant galaxy, through invading a terrorist-controlled country and making a full-budget cinema feature film, to sailing single-handedly around the world or planning a marriage.

All of these require the hours of preparation and training, the investment of considerable amounts of money, and large teams of back-up personnel.

They also search out the best equipment available with the money they have to spend. Sometimes money is no object. Sometimes *saving* money is the object.

The divine strategy is otherwise . . .

2. An insignificant solar system?

Let us begin with the heavens, in all their complexity and vastness. Among the 50 billion galaxies in the universe where a special and unique mission might be located, there are many magnificent and spectacular examples.

But, in our case, God selects a mediocre galaxy containing a mere 100 billion individual stars. And, instead of going straight to its shining centre, an average solar system, approximately halfway out, is chosen.

Let us look at the development of this solar system. It was born, approximately four billion years ago, out of a cloud of fine dust and gas, which, while circling the light of the sun, became boulders, which further fused into mountains, which became planets. At one stage, there may have been almost 100 planets vying violently for existence, destroying and absorbing each other, reducing numbers down to a bare handful. And yet, while there are several very large planets, God chooses one little sphere which should really have been swallowed up by the bigger ones or simply kicked out.

3. A fragile planet transformed

This little ball, despite all its fiery volcanoes, is then transformed, with masterly care, into an object of exquisite beauty. It becomes a living creature. Down below its "watery blue" atmosphere, there grows up an almost infinitely interwoven, but perfectly balanced, biodiversity of plant and animal life.

From a giant sequoia tree to a butterfly, from krill to a mountain range . . .

Such a seemingly fragile but immense work of genius surely deserves only the greatest protection.

God's strategy is otherwise.

4. Untrained guardians in charge

Very late in the day in the planet's life – towards the end of the 24th hour – God chooses to hand over the running of this paradise to a single species, a microcosmic version of his divine image.

Surely under careful parental control?

The divine strategy is otherwise.

If we take the skulls that have been unearthed in Africa and elsewhere, which show that our ancestors had a close resemblance to monkeys and apes, we can see that their primitive intellect was not exactly adequate for planet surveillance and care . . . and yet maybe, in their simplicity, they were able to do less harm.

5. A farming family survives

God chooses to give this species free will. This meant that, as with a child in a room filled with delicate glass and china, things could be broken. And they were.

After a while, God decides to begin again. He plans to drown it all – except for one single farming family, which he instructs to build a single boat to transport the biodiversity during a long-lasting and devastating flood. Not a fleet of boats, but a single vessel.

God's strategy is otherwise.

6. Ordinary little people

But even after this – despite the still, small voices crying in the wilderness – the child continues to break things. Yet, whenever he decides to help the child, God chooses those least likely, those with imperfections: the *"am ha" aretz* – people of the land, ordinary little people . . .

7. An extremely unlikely father (Genesis 12–25)

God had decided to make Abram "a great nation". But Abram was already 75 years old when he was told to leave his home in Haran, his family and his father's house, for a land he would be shown.

At first, Abram was an opportunist. His own wife, Sarai, was his father's daughter by another marriage. So, wherever they travelled, he would lie, claiming that she was only his sister. So two rulers, into whose lands they entered, fell in love with Abram's beautiful "sister" Sarai, heaping riches on Abram. When they discovered that Sarai was his wife, both of them "paid him off" before having him escorted out of their country.

As Sarai seemed destined to remain childless, her Egyptian maid, Hagar, bore the 86-year-old Abram a son, called Ishmael. He would become the ancestor of the twelve clans of Israel. Then God intervened. Firstly, he renamed Abram as Abraham, and Sarai as Sarah. When he told Abraham that Sarah would give him a son, Abraham bowed to the ground and he laughed, thinking to himself, "Is a child to be born to a man one hundred years old, and will Sarah have a child at the age of ninety?"

But a child she did have, whose name was Isaac. He became the ancestor of Jesus.

And after that, Abraham fathered six more sons by his third wife Keturah. They became the ancestors of the Arab tribes.

While Sarah lived to 127 years old, Abraham died at 175. They were buried alongside each other.

Through his children, Abraham is regarded as the father of Judaism, Christianity and Islam.

$8.$ A spoilt brother dreams dreams (Genesis 37–50)

Alongside the mighty Pharaoh, Joseph had become the most powerful chancellor in Egypt, even though he was not Egyptian.

During his youth in Canaan, he had been the favourite and spoilt son of the wealthy Jacob, who had presented him with a coat of many colours. Joseph was able to foresee the future in dreams. But Joseph's eleven brothers came to envy and hate him. One day, they threw him into an empty well and then sold him to Midianite slave traders heading for Egypt.

But God helped Joseph. He soon became the personal assistant of Potiphar, Pharaoh's commander of the guard. When he rejected an attempt by Potiphar's wife to seduce him, Joseph was thrown into prison. But even behind bars, Joseph was soon placed in charge of the prisoners' welfare. His ability to interpret dreams, particularly those of the mighty Pharaoh concerning the need to store up grain prior to a drought, persuaded Pharaoh to make Joseph his right-hand man.

Perhaps the least likely outcome was that when Joseph's brothers came to Egypt to buy some of this grain, it was Joseph who, at first unrecognised, "corrected" their behaviour before welcoming them with love.

$9.$ A reluctant leader (Exodus 1–4)

God decided to take the Israelites out of their captivity in Egypt. He could have chosen someone of influence, deeply involved in Egyptian politics. But instead he chose Moses, a long-term exile from Egypt, an alien in a foreign land, no more than a shepherd, and an aged one at that.

Even though God spoke from a burning bush and challenged Moses, the old man immediately expressed his inadequacy and concern that the Israelites would not believe him. Even after God had turned a staff into a snake and turned Moses' hand leprous, he still protested.

"Oh LORD, I have never been eloquent, neither in the past nor since you have spoken to your servant. I am slow of speech and not able to speak well."

God had to give him further encouragement.

"Who gave man his mouth? Who makes him deaf or mute? Is it not I, the LORD? Now go. I will help you speak and will teach you what to say."

In the drawn-out campaign against the might of Pharaoh, punctuated by a timely sequence of plagues, Moses showed himself well suited to the task, even to the point of commanding the sea itself to part so that the Israelites could cross over to the other side.

10. A prostitute is spared (Joshua 2 and 6)

Rahab was a prostitute in the city of Jericho.

One day, two spies arrived in the city to check out the lie of the land for their leader, Joshua. Although word had already gone around that the spies were in the city, Rahab hid them on the roof of her house under some stalks of flax. When the king of Jericho's men came to interrogate her, Rahab lied, telling them that the spies had already left. Before they really did leave, Rahab asked them to protect her and her father's house during the forthcoming siege. The spies agreed, telling her to hang a scarlet thread from her house as a sign.

Soon afterwards Joshua and his army circled the walls of

Jericho several times and blew their horns, and the city walls fell. But Rahab's house was spared.

In time, Rahab married Salmon. Their son Boaz married Ruth. Rahab's most important descendant would be Jesus of Nazareth.

11. The least important son (Judges 6–7)

The Midianites had dominated Israel for seven years. Something had to be done. An angel of the Lord visited a young man called Gideon, who was living in Ophrah. Gideon believed that the Lord had abandoned his people and given them into the clutches of the Midianites. When God told Gideon to go in his strength and save Israel, the young man protested, "Oh, my LORD, how will I save Israel? My family is poor in Manasseh, and I am the least in my father's house."

But God was with Gideon, and worked miraculous signs to give him confidence. So Gideon went off with an army of 32,000 men to fight the Midianites. But this was too many for God.

"Israel might claim credit for themselves at my expense; they might say, 'My own hand has rescued me.'"

So, on God's instructions, Gideon told anyone who was frightened or fearful to go home. Twenty thousand went home. But God still decided there were too many Israelites in the army, and, in a selection test which involved the way in which they drank by the waterside, Gideon's force was reduced to a mere 300 men. In a night attack near Mount Gilead, simply by using a psychological trick involving torches and horn-sounding, these men put the Midianites to flight . . . Gideon later became one of the greatest judges of Israel.

12. Boy versus giant warrior (1 Samuel 17)

Israel, led by King Saul, was in danger of being defeated by the superior army of the Philistines. They had a shock trooper among their ranks, a heavily armed giant called Goliath, from Gath. Every day this giant would mockingly challenge the Israelites to single combat on the condition that whoever lost, his country would be enslaved. Many experienced Israelite warriors feared the giant, and refused to rise to this challenge.

But then there was David, the youngest son of Jesse of Bethlehem. While his older brothers had become soldiers, young David had been left behind to look after his father's sheep. He also liked playing the harp. One day he was told to take some provisions to his brothers. When he saw Goliath shouting out his daily challenge, David protested, "Who is this uncircumcised Philistine, who dares insult the armies of the living God?" Summoned to an audience with King Saul, David volunteered to fight Goliath.

"You cannot go and fight the Philistine," Saul declared. "You are only a boy and he has been a warrior from his youth."

David explained that, while looking after his father's sheep, he had once had to kill a lion and on another occasion a bear, and that he placed his entire trust in God. Saul agreed, provided that David put on some good armour. But David found the armour too heavy. He was more at home with his simple slingshot and some smooth stones. With God's help, David killed Goliath with a single slingstone. Taking the enemy's sword, he cut off the giant's head. The Philistines retreated in fear.

In time, David would become the king of Israel.

13. Stowaway turned preacher (Jonah)

When the Lord asked Jonah, son of Amittai, to go to the great city of Nineveh and preach against its wickedness, Jonah ran away. From Tarshish he went to Joppa, and boarded a ship. During the journey, he told the ship's crew that he was running away from the Lord. So, when a storm blew up, they blamed Jonah. Jonah told them that, if they threw him overboard, the storm would die down. This is exactly what took place.

Then a great fish swallowed Jonah. He survived inside that fish for three full days. Once Jonah had agreed to work for God, the fish vomited him out on to dry land so he could go and prophesy.

Even then, Jonah was furious when the people of Nineveh repented and God forgave them.

14. A herdsman prophet (Amos)

Prophets do not have to be high priests, carefully trained in religious matters. Around 800 BC there lived a herdsman called Amos. He tended sheep near Tekoa, a small village in the hills, about twelve miles south of Jerusalem. Tekoa was located on the edge of the desert that slopes down towards the Dead Sea. A more desolate place is hard to imagine. The soil around the little town is very scant and shallow. Its poor vegetation obliged Amos to raise a peculiar breed of stunted, fine-wooled sheep. Small in size and ugly in appearance, they were highly esteemed for their wool. Amos supplemented his income by dressing an almost worthless fruit produced by sycamore trees. As Amos later declared, "I was neither a prophet nor a prophet's son. But the LORD took me from tending the flock and said to me, 'Go, prophesy to my people Israel.'"

So Amos went out and prophesied against the idolatry of the Israelites. His prophecies were so troubling that he was accused of conspiring against King Jeroboam.

15. A "child" commissioned (Jeremiah 1)

Jeremiah was the son of Hilkiah, a priest who was a native of Anathoth, two and a half miles north-west of Jerusalem. When the Lord God called Jeremiah and ordained him a prophet of the nations, he replied, "Ah, LORD God! Behold, I cannot speak; I am a child."

But the Lord said to him, "Say not, 'I am a child', for thou shalt go to all that I shall send thee, and whatsoever I command thee thou shalt speak. Be not afraid of their faces, for I am with thee to deliver thee."

16. The Servant Son (Gospels)

Wars, vengeance and hatred continued to poison the spirit of the creature whom God had regarded as his finest achievement. The prophets, it seemed, were not enough.

A long-considered choice is now made, where once again the odds are stacked heavily against success. God's strategy is to take what is dearest to him, his only Son, and to send him down with a message for the broken paradise.

But, instead of sending him down to a fully developed civilisation such as Egypt, Rome or China, God chooses his beloved, wayward group of desert tribes with their very chequered history of loyalty and reliability.

Instead of sending him down as the head of an invasion force of twelve legions of angels, he makes him into a solitary, vulnerable human being.

17. A man of many sorrows

Instead of selecting an influential and wealthy family to raise him, God chose a middle-aged carpenter and a teenage girl in a small village, in the wilds of a corrupt colony, in a cruel and powerful empire.

Instead of surrounding the mother with midwife and doctors, he chose the nocturnal isolation of a cave.

And when the child, called **Jesus**, became a man, following 40 days of gruelling fasting, he was given only 36 months to communicate his as yet unheard-of, non-violent message of love and forgiveness.

Surely the best scholars were there to act as witnesses. Surely there would be an accompanying scribe to carefully record this vital message for posterity?

God's strategy is otherwise.

Jesus' closest followers, the men he had to teach, were a doctor, some simple fishermen and several country youths. Then came a hardened tax-collector, and even a prostitute. Instead of mixing with the learned, the wealthy and the influential, he went around on foot, healing lepers, the crippled, blind beggars, even the insane – life's so-called dregs. He brought a teenage girl back to life, but then insisted that no-one else be told about it. He let a close friend die, and then brought him back to life to show the power of God, his father.

Instead of engaging in complex philosophical debates, he would tell simple stories about seed-growing, viticulture, shepherding and fishing. They often featured the least likely. He rarely entered temples and town squares, preferring fields and valleys, a mountain, a lake and a desert.

In a sermon preached on a mountain, he made a categorical statement in praise of the least likely: the poor in spirit, the gentle, those who mourn, the merciful, the pure in heart, the peacemakers, and those who are persecuted in the cause of right.

He valued wild flowers and little children – the simplest things.

Jesus' message is not one of military vengeance and bloody insurrection. It is one of non-violence, forgiveness and love.

He finally rode into a city which can rank among the bloodiest and most vengeful in history. Yet this was not the triumphal entry of a conquering general but that of a country teacher, in tears, on a young donkey. After his friends had betrayed, denied and abandoned him to a hurried, rigged and unfair trial, Jesus was tortured, crucified, lanced and asphyxiated.

Thus God allows this dearest part of himself to die. But then comes the masterstroke in this unequal, obstacle-stacked mission. He brings him back to life.

Yet even then, the first people to see him were women, and at first they mistakenly thought he was just the cemetery gardener. The Son does not remain for any length of time. Only weeks later, he is taken back to paradise. And, in his place, God sends an untouchable, invisible but very approachable Person, called the Holy Spirit.

Despite once tracing something in the sand with his finger, Jesus wrote nothing down. A total of only 50 days of his life would be recorded, and these almost half a century after they happened. If all his sayings were combined into one speech, it would not last longer than a few hours.

And yet, from this least likely of lives . . .

18. A very human fisherman (Matthew 14–16; Luke 5; Luke 22; Acts 2; 1 and 2 Peter)

Simon, son of Jonah, appeared to be the least likely man to champion any cause. A very ordinary fisherman, when Jesus told him to put out into deep water and let down the nets, Simon protested that they had been trying all night and had caught nothing. When those nets were full to breaking with fish, Simon told Jesus to go away, protesting that he was a sinful man.

Although Jesus gave Simon the new name of "Peter", for having identified him as the Christ, the Son of the living God, things still did not go smoothly.

When caught in a storm on the lake, Simon Peter lacked faith in Jesus and woke him up to calm the waters. When Jesus, walking on the water on another occasion, beckoned to Simon Peter to leave his boat and join him, halfway across he lost faith again and began to sink.

When Jesus was praying in the garden of Gethsemane, just before his arrest, Peter could not even stay awake to keep watch. Despite Jesus' message of non-violence, when the soldiers came to arrest him Peter took a sword and cut off the ear of one of them.

When Jesus had been taken prisoner for interrogation and torture, Peter publicly denied knowing him, three times. He was totally broken up at this betrayal and there is no record of his presence at the crucifixion.

But when Peter realised that Jesus Christ had risen from the dead, he became a changed man. On the day of the Pentecost, Peter, filled with the Holy Spirit, bravely spoke out so power-fully about his risen Master that some 3,000 people became believers on that day, increasing to 5,000 soon after. Subsequently, Peter went on several missionary voyages throughout Asia and wrote letters of encouragement to the fledgling Christian communities.

19. A traveller is baptised (Acts 8)

The conversions of some of the earliest Christians took place in the least likely situations. The northern portion of Ethiopia formed the kingdom of Meroe, which for a long period was ruled over by a series of queens. In the court of Queen Hindake, also known as Kandake, there was a eunuch who served as her chief treasurer. One day the eunuch was making a journey by chariot to Jerusalem. He was passing through the Gazan desert when he was approached by a Christian called Philip. They talked. He invited Philip to climb up onto the chariot. The journey continued, with Philip sharing the Good News of Jesus with him.

Still travelling, they came across a water hole. The eunuch asked Philip to baptise him then and there.

20. God uses a persecutor (Acts 9; 1 & 2 Corinthians)

The very first Christians found life very tough. Among those who hunted them down was a Jewish rabbi called Saul, born in Tarsus, Cilicia. As a zealous Pharisee, Saul went about "breathing out murderous threats" against Christians, arresting both men and women, and having them executed. He even went to the high priest and asked him for letters to the synagogues in Damascus, so that if he found any there who belonged to the Way, as the early Christians called it, he might take them as prisoners to Jerusalem. He was the least likely person to help them, let alone champion their cause.

But, on his journey to Damascus, suddenly a bright light from heaven flashed around him. He fell to the ground and heard a voice say to him, "Saul, Saul, why do you persecute me?"

"Who are you, LORD?" Saul asked.

"I am Jesus, whom you are persecuting," came the reply. "Now get up and go into the city, and you will be told what to do."

Having once gained the confidence of the Christians, Saul, now renamed Paul, was to go on three dangerous missionary voyages to proclaim the words of Christ. He would be beaten. He would be imprisoned. But he would write over a dozen inspiring letters to these fledgling communities, teaching them and encouraging them.

In the first long letter he wrote to the Corinthians, Paul showed his complete understanding of the way God works:

Brothers, think of what you were when you were called. Not many of you were wise by human standards; not many were influential; not many were of noble birth. But God chose the foolish things of the world to shame the wise; God chose the weak things of the world to shame the strong. He chose the lowly things of this world and the despised things—and the things that are not—to nullify the things that are, so that no-one may boast before him (1 Corinthians 1: 26–29).

Paul eventually arrived in Rome, where tradition has it that he was executed.

21. "How can I curse my King?"

Polycarp is said to have known the Apostle John and to have been instructed by him in the Christian faith. He was for a long time Bishop of Smyrna (today known as Izmir), a city on the west coast of Turkey.

In the year 155 AD, Polycarp was denounced by the government on the charge of being a Christian. At first, the fragile old man was persuaded by his friends to leave the city and conceal himself in a farmhouse. Here he spent his time in prayer. While praying, he fell into a trance in which he saw his pillow burning with fire: he told those that were with him, "It must needs be that I shall be burned alive."

When his pursuers came after him, Polycarp went to another farmhouse. Finding him gone, they tortured two slave boys, one of whom betrayed his place of hiding. Herod, head of the police, sent a body of men to arrest him on Friday evening. Escape was still possible, but the old man refused to flee, saying, "The will of God be done." He came down to meet his pursuers, had a friendly chat with them, and ordered food to be set before them. While they were eating, Polycarp prayed. Then he was led away. Herod and Herod's father, Nicetas, met him and took him into their carriage, where they tried to prevail upon him to save his life. Finding that they could not persuade him, they pushed him out of the carriage with such haste that he bruised his shin. He followed on foot till they reached the stadium, where a great crowd had assembled after having heard the news of his arrest.

Once in the stadium the proconsul urged the frail old man to save his life by cursing Christ. Bishop Polycarp replied, "Eighty-six years I have served him, and he never did me any wrong. How can I then curse my King who saved me?"

Polycarp was executed with a sword, and then burned.

22. A runaway slave

Around 190 AD, Callistus was a Roman slave, serving in the Christian household of Carpophorus. His master had entrusted large sums of money to Callistus to establish a bank for fellow Christians and widows.

After losing this money, the slave fled to Portus, pursued by his master. When Callistus, who had embarked on a ship, saw his master, he jumped into the sea to try to drown himself. But he was dragged ashore and condemned to the hand-mill, a harsh punishment reserved for slaves.

Following his release, and having insulted the Jews at their synagogue, Callistus was again condemned, this time to the mines in Sardinia. There he might have remained, had not Marcia, the mistress of the Emperor Commodus, persuaded Pope Victor to organise the release of Christian prisoners from those mines. Among them was Callistus.

Marcia's action must have had a strong effect on this former slave and criminal. In the years that followed, Callistus became a priest, then an archdeacon. Finally, he was pope for five years until his martyrdom in the year 223, after which his body was thrown into a well.

23. An oath too far

In 286 AD, the pagan Emperor Maximian went to eastern Gaul to suppress a revolt led by bandits and outlaws. Although he inflicted great slaughter, Maximian found the task formidable. So he sent for the Theban Legion. This task force had been trained in Egypt and was led by Maurus (= the Moor).

When Maurus arrived, he discovered that his emperor was not only carrying out a police action to secure loyalty to Rome, but also demanding a religious oath of subservience to pagan gods.

As a Christian, Maurus decided to withdraw, to avoid embarrassing his emperor. When the latter heard about this, he ordered a decimation, the execution of every tenth member of the 300-strong Theban Legion. Seeing that this made no difference, the furious emperor ordered a second decimation. Maurus and his Christian comrades moved up the Rhone and Rhine rivers, pursued by the emperor's men. They were eventually "run to ground" at Colonia Agrippina (present-day Cologne) and massacred.

Some say this is only a legend, but others say that it is based on fact. What *is* certain is that for centuries there were many churches consecrated in the name of Saint Maurus.

24. A wealthy martyr

The Roman Emperor Septimus Severus arrived in Britain probably around 208 AD. One of his first commands was the cruel persecution of all Christians. At the time, Alban was a wealthy resident of Verulamium, a city north of Londinium. He was loyal to his emperor and to the Roman deities. But then one day a priest called Amphibalus, pursued by the persecutor, appealed to Alban for help. Alban agreed to hide him. The priest's faith was so strong, even at this time of stress, that Alban was soon converted and became a follower of Jesus Christ.

After a few days, the civil government heard that Alban was sheltering a Christian fugitive in his house. Soldiers were sent. On arrival they were met by Alban, wearing the priest's clothes. They took him to the judge, who was furious. But because Alban was a Roman citizen, loyal to the emperor, he was offered freedom if he would make a sacrifice to a Roman deity. Alban refused.

He was scourged and tortured, but still he would not give up his new faith. He was then decapitated on a hill outside Verulamium.

Verulamium was renamed St Albans, and its cathedral houses Alban's shrine to this day, although his bones were removed in 1539.

25. A military emperor is baptised

Flavius Valerius Constantinus, a hardened soldier, had fought his way up to become Rome's sole emperor by 312. But, before the Battle of Milvian Bridge, in which his 20,000-strong army finally defeated his rival Maxentius, Constantine had seen a flaming cross in the sky inscribed: "In this, conquer". He had even ordered his warriors to carry Christ's monogram on their shields, although the majority of them were pagans.

Out of his gratitude to the God of the Christians, the victor immediately issued a new edict: Christian worship, hitherto cruelly suppressed, was henceforth to be tolerated throughout the Roman Empire (Edict of Milan, early in 313). Constantine even treated the conquered with magnanimity: no bloody executions followed his victory.

Although he continued to wage wars to defend his position, Constantine made Byzantium into his Christian capital. The Nicaean (or Nicene) Creed was worked out at a congress over which he presided.

Despite having executed his eldest son and his second wife

for treason, Constantine was baptised before his death at the age of 63.

26. From isolation to community

Pachomius was converted to Christianity shortly after completing his military service in Egypt, around 315 AD. Several years later, the young man decided to adopt the solitary and isolated life of a hermit at Tabennisi, beside the River Nile in Upper Egypt. Until then, the accepted way was for hermits to live near one another but never too close.

But Pachomius thought otherwise. He decided to assemble the other hermits in his locality as a Christian community, to pray together and to hold their goods in common. It was not easy. The first to join him was his own brother. At first Pachomius ran the community, leaving others to fast and pray. But in time a new ethos was born. The "monastery" at Tabennisi, though several times enlarged, became too small. A second was founded at Pabau, a third at Chenoboskion and, before Pachomius died, there were eleven monasteries, including two for women.

Pachomius is regarded as the founder of the many thousands of monasteries and nunneries which have since welcomed the world of humanity into communal spiritual life.

27. "Confessions" of an intellectual

The son of a heathen lawyer based in Numidia, Augustine had thoroughly enjoyed the high life in Carthage, northern Africa. Before he was 18, his mistress had given him a son. He was fascinated by the tenets of the Manichean sect, and indeed by any other philosophical writings. After taking his common-law family to Milan, Augustine began to attend the sermons preached by Ambrose, the local bishop. They became friends. At first, Augustine would not let go of his love of intellectualism and sensuality.

An inner conflict built up. Then one day he accepted Jesus, and in 387 AD Ambrose baptised him and his son, Adeodatus. Augustine abandoned his teaching post, and sent his mistress away. Four years later he became a priest, and wrote several books in the years that followed in the town of Hippo, North Africa. One of them, *Confessions*, would have a profound influence on the spirit of the Christian church for centuries to come. The Augustinian Order is named after him.

28. A disenchanted teenager

For three years, the 16-year-old boy had been living in seclusion in a cave near Subiaco, south-east of Rome. He had abandoned his expensive classical education in that city, disgusted by its heathen immorality. Benedict wore nothing but a sheepskin and was cared for by a monk called Romanus. When word got round about the teenager's piety, he was invited to become abbot of a nearby monastery. But even then, he left, because the morals of the half-wild monks were not strict enough for him.

As many people continued to seek him out for guidance, Benedict eventually founded twelve small communities with twelve monks in each. Ultimately he moved to Monte Cassino, about 80 miles south east of Rome. There he destroyed the pagan temple dedicated to Apollo, and built his first monastery. It was here, in about 515, that he wrote his

Regula Monachorum, which laid down the rules for monastery life, which involved manual labour, teaching young people, and copying manuscripts for the library.

Today, the Benedictine Order comprises many hundreds of monasteries and many thousands of monks and nuns.

29. A reluctant bishop

In 875 AD, when the Vikings began to invade Britain, the Christian monks of the island monastery of Lindisfarne did a strange thing. They dug up the body of a former bishop who had died some 200 years before and, carrying it on their shoulders, they fled inland. From then on, for the next 100 years, the mortal remains of St Cuthbert wandered with the displaced monks until, finally, they were interred in Durham Cathedral. Throughout that time, they were said not to have decayed.

In the year 684, a 50-year-old hermit and former plague victim by the name of Cuthbert was living in a self-built cell with a single window on the isolated, infertile islet of Inner Farne, in northern Britain. Strange legends had already grown up about his life. One evening he was praying by the ocean, and the waters rose up and swamped him. The next day he was washed ashore, chilled but still praising God. Then sea otters came and warmed him, and comforted him and washed his feet, and he gave them his blessing.

As a limping teenage shepherd boy, Cuthbert had received a vision of angels which made him resolve to become a monk. For this he was educated by Irish monks at Melrose Abbey, and later became a prior at the Abbey of Lindisfarne, a small island joined to the coast at low tide. From there he had gone on many rugged journeys, humbly telling the people of

Northumbria about Jesus Christ – until he decided to become a hermit. Indeed, Cuthbert was only persuaded to leave his hermitage and become a bishop by the king of Northumbia. Despite ill health, he administered his see, cared for those in his region who suffered from the plague, distributed alms liberally, and worked so many miracles of healing that he was known in his lifetime as the "wonder-worker of Britain". But he did not stay away for long, returning to die on Inner Farne two years later.

Cuthbert was particularly interested in the habits of birds and beasts. His influence remains even today. The Farne Islands are now a bird and wildlife sanctuary. And there are over 130 churches named after St Cuthbert.

30. A pagan prince destroys his idols

During the last quarter of the 10th century, Vladimir was Grand Prince of Kiev. Here was a man reared on idolatry, who had seven wives and numerous female slaves, and who had erected idols and pagan temples and participated in idolatrous rites, possibly involving human sacrifice.

In about 987 the Byzantine Emperor Basil II, then aged only eleven, sought military aid from Vladimir. The two sealed a pact for aid that involved Basil's sister Anna being given to Vladimir in marriage – and Vladimir becoming a Christian. At first it was merely a political measure, and Vladimir hesitated a great deal.

But once he had truly accepted Christ into his life, he did not look back. He was baptised, took the patronal name Basil, and then ordered the Christian conversion of Kiev and Novgorod. Idols were thrown into the River Dnieper. He built churches, monasteries and schools, and brought in Greek and

German missionaries to educate his people. He greatly reduced capital punishment, and gave lavish alms to the poor.

Vladimir died in 1015 after giving all his personal belongings to his friends and the poor. He was later made Patron Saint of Russia.

31. A migraine sufferer sees visions

In the 12th century, alongside the Benedictine monastery of Disibodenberg there stood a hermit-like convent comprising small cells with single windows. Among those living there was a teenage girl named Hildegard. In her isolation, all she was expected to do was to learn the Psalms in Latin, pray, then stitch or embroider, all under the strict control of an anchoress by the name of Jutta.

During the next 20 years, until she became abbess of that convent, Hildegard suffered terribly from what today are recognised as migraines. But, whenever she suffered, she received extraordinary visions. At first she felt that as an obedient nun she should keep her visions to herself. But eventually, in 1140, she decided to have 35 of them written down and illuminated in a book called *Scivias*, which means "Know the Ways of the Lord". She then went on to write music to accompany part of the book.

By the time she died, in 1179 aged 81, Hildegard had completed two more books, one on natural history, and one on medicine, and written the music and lyrics to over 50 hymns. She preached that man was the peak of God's creation, the microcosmic mirror through which the splendour of the macrocosm was reflected. She moved her swelling convent to Bingen on the Rhine, where several of her mystery plays had been performed. She even invented a coded language with nearly a thousand words and 23 letters. Her fame spread beyond her native Germany: she exchanged letters with bishops, popes and kings, and travelled extensively.

Her migraines never left her. Nor did her visions.

Some 800 years later, Hildegard von Bingen's life and work have been re-discovered. Over a dozen books have been published about her, and her music has been recorded on several CDs, providing calm and serenity.

32. A wealthy playboy embraces poverty

Giovanni Bernadone was the son of a wealthy merchant in Assisi, Umbria. Loving the life and carefree style of the wandering minstrels and poets, he soon received the nickname "il Francesco" (the little Frenchman). He would spend his money lavishly, but mostly on himself. At one point Francesco bought himself expensive armour and a horse and rode off to take part in a military expedition. But, en route, he met a man reduced to poverty and raggedly dressed. Francesco was so touched with compassion that he exchanged clothes with the pauper. That night he had a dream about a rich palace, filled with weapons but all marked with the sign of the cross. He returned home and began to devote himself to the care of the poor and the sick, even lepers. He gave up his inheritance, including even the clothes he wore, and became a hermit. He was 25 years old.

By 1210 Francesco of Assisi had founded a small brotherhood of eleven, based on chastity, poverty and obedience. By 1219 there were some 5,000 Franciscan monks. So intense was Francesco's devotion to Christ that he received the excruciatingly painful stigmata, the marks of the wounds that Jesus suffered during his crucifixion.

33. Misguided child crusaders

The Crusades were a misguided and bloody series of military campaigns intended to regain Jerusalem from Islamic control "in the name of Jesus Christ". Perhaps the least likely of these Crusades began in 1212.

A twelve-year-old shepherd boy called Stephen, from the French village of Cloyes in the Vendôme region, was approached by a beggar who claimed to be a poverty-stricken Crusader returning from Palestine. Stephen gave him a small crust of bread, whereupon the beggar revealed himself as "Jesus Christ". Soon afterwards, Stephen persuaded King Philip of France to let him lead the next Crusade. The difference was that the Crusaders were to be an army of children, aged from six to 18, with innocence as their armour. By the summer of 1212, a staggering 30,000 young people are said to have assembled at Vendôme to begin their journey to Jerusalem, via the port of Marseilles.

Unknown to Stephen, at the same time a ten-year-old German boy called Niklaus had assembled another 20,000 people to march to the Holy Land.

Tragically, thousands of the French child Crusaders died en route; hundreds were drowned during the voyage and countless others were sold into slavery, a number of them being beheaded for refusing to become Muslims. The German Crusaders either died crossing the Alps or were persuaded by the then Pope, Innocent III, to abandon their Crusade. Only 2,000 of the 20,000 ever reached their homeland again. Although the Pope did not officially sanction the Children's Crusade, he did not forbid it either.

34. A housewife set apart

In 1393, at 20, Margery Kempe married a businessman in the small town of Lynn in eastern England. She bore him no less than fourteen children.

When she was about 35, she had a vision and felt that she had been "called from the pride and vanity of this wretched world". She began to live an ascetic life and tried to avoid sexual relations with her husband. It took about five years, but John Kempe eventually agreed to live with his wife without sexual contact.

Five years later, in 1413, Margery made the courageous decision to go on long-distance pilgrimages. At the time, visiting the tomb of St Thomas à Becket in Canterbury was considered adventurous. But Margery travelled to Jerusalem and Rome, then to Santiago de Compostela in Spain. Twenty years later, having nursed her dying husband, she made further hazardous pilgrimages to Trondheim in Norway, to Cologne in Germany and to Gdansk in Poland.

Although illiterate, Margery Kempe dictated her memoirs in a book which runs to 99 chapters.

35. A desperate widow embraces peace

Rita Lotti had taken about all she could suffer. In the year 1412, her husband by an arranged marriage, Paolo Mancini, watchman at Roccaporena village, near Cascia, Italy, was ambushed and brutally murdered as part of a city vendetta. Despite her prayers, Rita's two sons were killed within the year while trying to avenge their father. When the desperate widow asked to enter the nearby Augustinian convent at

Cascia, she was rejected three times. She had been too close to the political infighting.

Only when Rita had persuaded her late husband's family to stop warring, forgive their enemies and sign a document to that effect, was she admitted to the convent. As Sister Rita, she would remain there for 40 years. Aged 62, a strange wound appeared in her forehead, which some said was "as if from a thorn in the crown that had covered Jesus' own head".

36. A German monk preaches salvation by faith

In the early 1500s, a brilliant young German graduate by the name of Martin Luther was planning to become a lawyer. But then the course of his life was changed by a series of events that included an illness, an accident, the death of a close friend, and a violent thunderstorm in which he nearly lost his life when struck by lightning.

As a result of all this, Martin decided to give up "the world", as he called it, and devote himself and his whole life to serving God. Since he knew of no other way of doing this than by becoming a monk, in 1505 he entered the Erfurt Monastery, home to the Augustinian hermits, an order famous for its scholarship. It was there, aged 22, that he saw a Bible for the first time. It was in Latin. A strict daily schedule, dictating spiritual and ascetic exercises and further scientific education within the order, was to control his life as a monk for many years.

Two years later Martin was ordained a priest by the Roman Catholic Church, then the only Christian church in Europe. After this he went to Wittenberg, where he became a powerful and influential preacher of philosophy and the Scriptures.

It might well have remained that way.

But then, on a mission to Rome in 1510, Martin was appalled by the financial corruption that he found. They were selling indulgences or "passages to heaven" to pay for the rebuilding of St Peter's Cathedral. Instead of falling into line with such a policy, Luther returned to Wittenberg where he began to preach the reformed doctrine of salvation by faith rather than works. In 1517, he openly published his criticisms by nailing an accusing document onto the door of Wittenberg Church. This included denying the Pope the right to forgive sins. Luther's attacks on the Holy See increased from then on, despite official demands and threats that he withdraw. His offences included translating the Bible into German. In 1524, Martin Luther married Katherina von Bora, a nun who had withdrawn from convent life.

This former hermit had sparked off the Reformation and caused the birth of the Protestant Church, to which many millions of Christians belong today.

37. An injured nobleman reads about Jesus

In 1521, Inigo Lopez de Recalde, a soldier of noble birth, was recuperating in the family castle in Loyola, northern Spain from a severe war wound to his right leg. The accompanying fever had nearly robbed him of his life. To pass the time, the frail de Recalde asked for some reading matter. Romances would do. But there were no romances – only a book about the life of Jesus and other legends of the saints. At first he read them merely to while away the time.

But God had his hand on this young Spaniard. Before long he was planning a pilgrimage to Jerusalem. En route he stopped to serve the poor and sick, and then withdrew to a cavern where he fasted until, utterly exhausted, he was carried back to hospital. Having recovered again, he made the pilgrimage. Then, in 1534, with six associates he founded the Society of Jesus. To be known to history as Ignatius Loyola, Inigo and his Jesuits vowed to go as missionaries to any country the Pope might choose.

From 1,000 Jesuits and 150 foundations at his death in 1556, the Jesuit Order grew until 100 years later there were 15,000 members and 550 foundations, spread throughout Europe, the Far East and America.

38. A sickly boy king makes his mark

Edward Tudor was only nine years old when he became King Edward VI of England. Suffering from tuberculosis, the boy was so weak that politicians had to govern for him. Yet this teenage monarch had an advisor and close friend in Nicholas Ridley, the Bishop of London. In 1553, Ridley pleaded with the king to establish institutions to care for the sick, needy and destitute children in strife-torn London. The result was the setting up of three hospitals: the Hospital of St Thomas the Apostle, Christ's Hospital, and Bridewell Royal Hospital, which Ridley saw as a place "which would wonderfully serve to lodge Christ in".

In addition, Edward not only gave his support to a "Book of Common Prayer", but he also founded many grammar schools, including ones at Sherborne in Dorset and Bromsgrove in Worcestershire.

Although Edward died aged only 15, and Ridley was burned at the stake by Edward's Catholic sister several years later, those hospitals and schools are still in existence over 450 years later.

39. Butcher's wife "pressed to death"

Margaret Middleton was the daughter of a respectable candle-maker in the city of York, England. Hers was a Protestant family, and, owing to the recent destruction of England's Catholic educational system, she was taught neither to read nor to write. When Margaret was 15, she married John Clitherow, a wealthy York butcher and respected Anglican.

About three years after their wedding, Margaret secretly returned to the Catholic religion of her forebears. At the same time, her husband professed his Protestant faith and became a city chamberlain. Despite this, Margaret sent their son to be educated among Catholics in Douai, France. She made their home into a stopping-off place for Catholic priests. But before long she was discovered and arrested. She was 30 years old, and pregnant. To keep her family out of it, she refused to plead. Reluctantly, the judge sentenced her to be "pressed to death". She was placed under a door, and rocks were piled onto the door until she was crushed.

Margaret died on 25th March 1586, her last words being "Jesu, Jesu, Jesu, have mercy on me!"

In 1970, she became Saint Margaret Clitherow.

40. Cheerful boy sings at his own crucifixion

The Jesuit missionaries working in Japan during the 1580s won thousands of converts, and at first believed that they would be tolerated. But then Japan's absolute ruler, General Toyotomi Hideyoshi, changed his mind and decreed that all missionaries must leave the realm.

None of the 100 Jesuits obeyed this order, and instead they

went underground to continue to serve and comfort the Japanese Catholics. To set an example, Hideyoshi ordered that a symbolic number of Christians resistant to Shintoism and Buddhism be arrested in Kyoto: six Franciscan friars, 17 Japanese converts and three Jesuits. Their left ears were cut off as a sign of disgrace, and then they were forcibly marched through town after town for 30 days in the cold mid-winter, as a warning to other would-be Christians. Their destination was Nagasaki, where ready-made crosses awaited them.

Among the teenagers was twelve-year-old Louis Ibaraki. Although he was not one of the original group that was arrested, he had been part of the entourage that accompanied it on the march. Louis had only tagged along to help the prisoners, one of whom was his uncle. But then Louis became part of the death march. He endeared himself to all by his constant laughter and singing, even when they cut off his ear. He even sang at his own crucifixion alongside the other martyrs, on 5th February 1597.

41. Erotic poet turned priest

1630: St Paul's Cathedral, London. Huge congregations had been assembling regularly to hear the sermons preached by their popular Dean, the Very Reverend John Donne, and to sing his inspiring hymns.

Could this be the same John Donne who, as an impoverished and rather cynical poet, used to write of his sexual experiences in religious terms, and of his devotional experience in erotic terms? And who, following his illicit marriage to a 16-year-old, had been thrown out of his job and imprisoned, coming out to face years of debt and illness?

But then his poems had begun to change, with titles such as

"To God, My God, in my Sicknesse". A former Catholic, John Donne had been ordained priest in the Anglican Church.

Yes, it was the very same.

42. Puritan settler amid "heathen savages"

When the Puritan "Pilgrim Fathers" first arrived in New England in the 1630s, among them was a young priest called John Eliot. For several years he simply preached to the settlers in the church at Roxbury. After all, many considered the surrounding tribes – the Massachusett, the Wampanoag, the Pennacook and others – as mere "heathen savages".

Not so John Eliot. Following the instructions to spread the gospel to all nations, in 1646 he began to learn the culture and native language of the local Wampanoag – Algonquin. Then he started to tell them about Jesus. In the years that followed, John Eliot made first a catechism and then the Bible available to them in their own language. It was called *Mamusse Wunnetupanatawe Up-Biblium God.*

He then planned missions where his Indian Christians could live using their own languages, culture and laws, calling these "Praying Indian Missions". The first was at Natick under the rule of the Massachusetts Bay colony. One of the first Indians to be converted at Natick was Daniel Takawambpait, who was later ordained a minister. There were thousands of Christians among the 14 Praying Indian Missions established: Punkapoag, Hassanamesit, Okommakamesit, Wamesit, Nashoba and Magunkaquog.

Sadly these were scattered and gradually reduced by warfare. It would be a long time before the Christian Indians would reunite.

43. Brilliant mathematician submits to Jesus Christ

An infant prodigy, trained by his mathematician father, Blaise Pascal went on to become a brilliant mathematician and physicist. He invented a calculating machine, a barometer, an hydraulic press and a syringe, and developed differential calculus. But he cared little for religious beliefs, unlike his sister, Jacqueline, who had entered a convent.

Then on the night of 23rd November 1654, Blaise, at 31 years old, had a deeply mystical experience in which he discovered the truth of the Christian faith. "Renonciation totale et douce. Soumission totale à Jésus-Christ," (*Total, sweet renunciation; submission to Jesus Christ*) he wrote in a paper discovered after his death, sewn into the lining of his coat.

He joined his sister in her retreat and devoted a great deal of the remaining five years of his short life to studying and writing on Christian doctrines.

Blaise Pascal was once asked why he believed in eternal salvation or eternal life. He made this reply:

> Let us assume that I am wrong and there is no life hereafter – then I have lost nothing. On the other hand, let us assume that I am right and there is life hereafter, then I have gained everything.

Fragments jotted down for a book of Christian truth were discovered after his death and published as *Pensées sur la Religion (Thoughts on Religion)*.

44. Chaplain identifies with plague victims

In the early 1660s, bubonic plague spread throughout Europe, devastating its population. No village was spared. It arrived, for example, at Eyam in Derbyshire, England, carried by fleas hiding in a box of damp cloth brought up from London for the village tailor. Up until that time, Eyam had been a flourishing rural community – so much so that, two years before, a brilliant young Cambridge undergraduate by the name of William Mompesson had been sent from a comfortable position as domestic chaplain to the wealthy Sir George Savile to take up his duties in the rectory of Eyam.

When the first plague victims were noticed in the village, Mompesson could have left with the others. He decided to stay. To prevent the plague from spreading to neighbouring communities, he instructed the villagers not to stray beyond the parish boundaries, with food from outside being left in wells, or troughs of running water, along the parish boundary. Mompesson even preached in the open air to avoid infection.

Of the 350 or so who had remained in the village, only 83 survived. Mompesson's wife was among the victims. Once the frost had killed off the plague fleas, Mompesson stayed on at Eyam for three years to help those who remained to rebuild their shattered community.

45. A wild young man authors Christian bestseller

John Bunyan, son of a tinker and brazier in a small village near Bedford in England, was originally trained in his father's profession. He was educated at the village school and, like most wild young men, thought nothing of swearing, drinking, dancing and gambling. But then he married a poor girl who brought with her two books that had belonged to her father. One of them was called *The Plain Man's Pathway to Heaven*. This was the start of John Bunyan's personal journey home to Jesus. He began to preach in the surrounding villages. Indeed, he never really left the Bedford area. He wrote a series of small religious books, and was twice imprisoned for his strict religious outlook during the licentious reign of King Charles II.

It was during his second period in prison, which lasted six months, that Bunyan wrote the first part of *The Pilgrim's Progress, From This World To That Which Is To Come*. This is an allegory of "Christian's" journey from the City of Destruction to the Celestial City. This book, beautifully and simply written, was first published in 1678. The extraordinary appeal that it makes to the human mind is shown by its success. In the first ten years, its sales totalled 100,000. For the next two and a half centuries it remained a bestseller. Within the first hundred years some 160 editions had been issued. It was also translated into more than 200 foreign languages and dialects. It is still widely in print today, and available on the Internet.

$46.$ A determined tutor makes a vital discovery

Jean de La Bruyère was in his forties when, as an influential Parisian writer and teacher of the dauphin, the future king of France, he set about translating *Characters*, the work of the Greek philosopher Theophrastus, into French. In the second part of his book, published in 1688, La Bruyère presented a collection of maxims, reflections and character portraits of the time.

In section 16 of his book, the French moralist makes a profound remark:

L'impossibilité où je suis de prouver que Dieu n'est pas, me découvre son existence. (The impossibility, from where I am, of proving that God does not exist, reveals his existence to me.)

$47.$ Writer in the saddle

In 1738, two young university graduates, John and Charles Wesley, returned to England from Governor James Oglethorpe's colony of Georgia in America, feeling that they had failed in their mission of teaching the Indian tribes about the Gospel of Christ. Sons of the rector of the village church of Epworth, both felt that they had missed their goal of doing great things for God.

John Wesley was convinced that the only place to preach from was a pulpit inside a church. But then, through a sequence of spiritual experiences, Wesley was one day led to preach a sermon in the open air to a company of coal miners. From then on, for the next 50 years, John Wesley preached his "Methodist" doctrine of justification by faith – "in the fields". His simple approach offended many parish ministers, who closed their pulpits to him. He preached twice a day, sometimes four times, sometimes more. Wesley's sermons were often interrupted. Sometimes cows were driven into the crowd, and often he had to overcome hostile mobs.

It is estimated that he travelled almost 5,000 miles a year, mostly on horseback, but also on foot. He did not ride rapidly because he studied and wrote as he went. He even studied several foreign languages. Indeed he became so comfortable in the saddle that, whenever he was writing on the ground, he preferred to use a special chair, facing backwards, which replicated his position on horseback! He also crossed the Irish Sea 42 times.

During his many journeys, groups of up to 30,000 people would wait patiently for hours just to hear him preach. They were mostly from working-class neighbourhoods – colliers, miners, foundrymen, weavers and day-labourers in towns.

John Wesley wrote a staggering 3,000 books and pamphlets

on varied subjects, earning £30,000, which he distributed to charity. His brother Charles, who acted as his lieutenant, wrote over 5,000 hymns.

Their legacy is the worldwide Methodist Church.

48. Former slave trader writes hymns

"Amazing Grace", "How Sweet the Name of Jesus Sounds", "One There is Above All Others", and several other unforgettable hymns were written in the 1760s by John Newton, an evangelical curate in the town of Olney in Buckinghamshire, England. They are still sung by Christians today, 250 years later.

Yet John Newton was not always a committed Christian. At the age of eleven he went to sea and spent the next 20 years as a sailor, engaged in the cruel trade of capturing Africans, shipping them in chains across the Atlantic and selling them as slaves. His life was spent in the lowest sort of wickedness. At one time he himself was the property of an African woman, who fed him only that which she threw under her table.

"I saw the necessity of religion as a means of escaping Hell," he wrote later, "but I loved sin, and was unwilling to forsake it."

He was nearly killed several times during terrible storms at sea. During one of those storms his wicked life passed before him, and deep conviction caused him to cry out to God for salvation. The next several years were spent in preparation for the ministry. He learned Latin, Greek and Hebrew, and studied the Scriptures intensively. In 1764 John Newton was appointed rector of the little parish of Olney and, helped by a poet called William Cowper, began to write hymns. In later life he would become a supporter of the anti-slavery movement.

49. A village shoemaker with a big vision for mission

As a young village shoemaker with a thirst for learning, William Carey kept a map of the world on the wall of his workshop so that he could pray for all nations. He was an avid reader, and, following his discovery of *The Last Voyage of Captain Cook*, he received a burning desire to spread the gospel abroad. But this was in the 1790s in the middle of rural England. There were no missionary societies, and indeed one older minister admonished Carey for his zeal: "Young man, sit down; when God pleases to convert the heathen, he will do it without your aid or mine."

But God *had* chosen. Carey did not give up. He wrote and published *An Enquiry Into the Obligations of the Christians to Use Means for the Conversion of the Heathen.* In this masterpiece on missions, Carey answered arguments, surveyed the history of missions from apostolic times, surveyed the entire known world as to countries, size, population and religions, and dealt with the practical application of how to reach the world for Christ!

A Baptist Missionary Society was set up soon afterwards. Carey and his wife and child made the voyage to India. There were years of discouragement (no Indian convert for seven years), debt, disease, deterioration of his wife's mind, death, but by the grace of God – and by the power of the Word – Carey never gave up.

When he died in 1834, at the age of 73, he had seen the Scriptures translated and printed into 40 languages. He had been made a college professor, and had founded a college at Serampore. He had seen India open its doors to missionaries. He had seen an edict passed to prohibit *sati* (burning widows on the funeral pyres of their dead husbands). And he had seen Hindus become Christians.

On his deathbed, Carey called out to a missionary friend, "Dr Duff! You have been speaking about Dr Carey; when I am gone, say nothing about Dr Carey – speak about Dr Carey's God."

50. Hairdresser leaves a legacy

During the 1790s, Pierre Toussaint, a Haiti-born black slave, became a hairdresser for the wealthy of New York City. Apart from giving them the latest hairstyle, he became known for helping his clients to find solutions to their problems in the gospel, through prayer and trust in God. Although Toussaint received a handsome income from working 18 hours a day, instead of buying his own freedom, he used his money to support the church, the poor and orphaned, and even for buying freedom for other slaves.

When his owner, Monsieur Jean Bérard, died of pleurisy, Toussaint discreetly supported his widow. He even postponed his own wedding until Madame Bérard's death. Although themselves childless, Pierre and Juliette Toussaint went on to shelter many orphans, refugees and other unfortunate people in their tiny flat. He co-founded one of New York City's first orphanages. During an epidemic of yellow fever, while thousands fled the city, the Toussaints stayed behind to nurse the sick. He and his wife donated funds for New York's first Catholic school for blacks.

When Pierre Toussaint died in 1853, a friend said of him, "I have known Christians who were not gentlemen, gentlemen who were not Christians. One man I know who is both, and that man is black."

51. Carpenter finds a living faith

At the end of the 18th century in Scandinavia, churchgoing was as conventional as anywhere else. The right to preach the gospel was legally restricted to ordained clergy in the Lutheran Church of Norway, who were also civil servants. A law had been passed, called the Conventicle Act, which maintained this status quo.

Hans Nielsen Hauge had little formal education, but was a skilled carpenter and repairman, and was therefore economically secure. He had been reared in a devout home in rural Norway, some 50 miles from Oslo. As a young man, he did much religious reading, and became deeply worried that he might be damned. While working on his father's farm, on 5th April 1796, just two days after he turned 25, Hans had a mystical experience. He suddenly felt assured of his salvation and called to share his assurance with others. He began to travel through Norway and Denmark, preaching everywhere about "the living faith", the personal relationship with the Lord that transforms the believer's life.

In this, he was flouting the Conventicle Act. In an attempt to stop him, Hans was arrested no fewer than ten times, and was finally imprisoned in 1804. Five years later, he was released to work on a project to extract salt from the ocean, and then imprisoned again. In 1811 he was permitted to return to farming, but in 1813 he was arrested and imprisoned once more for preaching. During this time, he wrote on the subject of faith, producing about 30 religious tracts. When finally released, he married twice; his first wife died soon after their marriage, and three of his four children died in infancy. By this time, Hans Nielsen Hauge had the friendship and support of several bishops, but his health and his spirit were broken, and his confidence in his mission weakened. He died on 29th March 1824.

52. Hindu carpenter becomes a preacher of the gospel

As the 19th century approached, there were few indigenous Christians on the Indian sub-continent. The predominant religion was Hinduism, which involved the worship of gods such as Krishna.

Krishna Pal was a poor Hindu carpenter, renting his land and hut, his earning capacity limited by his asthma, who worked long hours to support his wife, sister-in-law, four daughters and adopted son.

On 25th November 1800, Krishna Pal dislocated his right shoulder. Dr John Thomas, the first missionary to India from the Baptist Missionary Society, set the Hindu carpenter's shoulder, and, through an interpreter, spoke to him about the Christian faith. Several weeks later, Krishna Pal became the first Hindu to give his life to Christ. William Carey baptised him in the Ganges River.

Krishna Pal became a pastor and preached the gospel for more than 20 years, as well as authoring several Christian hymns.

53. Outcast bandit transformed

Jager Afrikaner was an Oorlam (a Hottentot) bandit of Namaqualand, an outcast who lived by raiding cattle and ter-rorising farmers in the wilds of Namibia (South-West Africa). In 1810 he even went as far as to attack the London Missionary Society mission at Pella. He was such a hardened character that the governor at Cape Town had offered 500 dollars for him, dead or alive.

Then Afrikaner was persuaded to accept a German missionary, the Reverend Johannes Ebner, into his clan. In June 1815 Ebner baptised Jager and his family and from then on Jager became known as a Christian. Three years later the Reverend Ebner took Robert Moffat, a fellow missionary from the London Missionary Society, to visit Afrikaner. A farmer they passed on the way warned them about the desperate character of the man they were going to visit. He told Moffat that he was taking his life into his hands by going near Afrikaner, asserting that Afrikaner would use his skull as a drinking cup.

At first Afrikaner was cool and reserved towards Moffat. But gradually a strong personal friendship grew. Afrikaner took a keen interest in what the missionary taught, attended the worship services and learned to read the Bible and to write. His way of life was so changed that in 1819 Moffat persuaded Afrikaner to accompany him to Cape Town. Afrikaner was wary at first because he knew that there was a price of 500 dollars on his head. On the way to Cape Town, Moffat spent the night at the home of a farmer named Engelbrecht, who was amazed to see that he was still alive after visiting the outlaw. As nothing had been heard of the missionary, people feared that the outlaw chief had ordered his death. Afrikaner was introduced to the farmer, who raised his eyes heavenwards and said in amazement, "O God, what a miracle of thy power! What cannot thy grace accomplish!"

54. An invalid hymn-writer

As a young woman in Brighton, England, Miss Elliott was known as "carefree Charlotte". She was a popular portrait artist and a writer of humorous verse. In 1805, at 16 years of age, she was visiting some friends in the west end of London, and there met the well-known Swiss evangelist, Dr Cesar Malan. While seated at supper, the minister said he hoped that she was a Christian. She took offence at this, and replied that she would rather not discuss that matter. Dr Malan said that he was sorry if he had offended her, but that he always liked to speak a word for his Master, and that he hoped that the young lady would some day become a worker for Christ. When they met again at the home of a mutual friend, three weeks later, Miss Elliott told the minister that ever since he had spoken to her, she had been trying to find her Saviour, and that she now wished him to tell her how to come to Christ. "Just come to him as you are," Dr Malan said.

Fourteen years passed. At the age of 30, a serious ailment made Charlotte Elliott an invalid for life. Despite being bed-ridden, she began to write hymns. The first echoed the advice of Dr Malan:

> With many a conflict, many a doubt,
> Fightings and fears within, without,
> O Lamb of God, I come, I come.

The other facet to this story is that Charlotte Elliott wrote this text and published it to aid a building fund, the building being a school for the children of poor clergy. In the end, this one hymn brought in more funds than all the other fundraising projects combined. In all, she would write 150 hymns, and is today regarded as one of the greatest hymn-writers of all time.

55. Women of colour

In 1791 there had been an uprising by the slaves on the island of Santo Domingo. Among those free "people of colour" who fled the island was a well-educated French-speaking, Catholic young woman, not without means, called Elizabeth Lange. Arriving in Baltimore, in the slave-holding state of Maryland, Miss Lange defiantly set about teaching black refugee children, even though the education of slaves was then against the law.

After ten years, Elizabeth Lange and her colleagues ran out of money. It was then that the Catholic Archbishop of Baltimore challenged Elizabeth to establish a religious congregation. On 2nd July 1828, Elizabeth and three other "women of colour" met to pronounce simple vows of obedience. This established the first order of African-American nuns in the history of the Catholic Church. Elizabeth became the first mother superior of the Oblate Sisters of Providence and took the name Mary.

At this time there were still theologians in Rome declaring that black people had no souls. Some Catholics thought it disgraceful that black women should wear a "holy habit". There were those who threatened the sisters physically.

Despite this, the Oblate Sisters educated black youths and provided a home for orphans of the Civil War. Freed slaves were educated and at times admitted into the order. They nursed the terminally ill in their almshouses during the cholera epidemic of 1832, sheltered the elderly, and even served as domestics at St Mary's Seminary in times of crisis.

When the Order fell on hard times in the 1840s, Elizabeth took in washing and ironing to support the sisters and orphans. The then Archbishop of Baltimore was a native Marylander. His family were slave owners. Seeing the poverty of the sisters, he ordered them to disband the community and become servant girls. Mother Mary Elizabeth refused. One can only imagine how "shocked" the Catholic population were when they learned that a black woman had refused to obey a white bishop.

Mother Mary Elizabeth Lange died at the age of 98 in 1882.

56. A dying pastor is inspired

On 4th September 1847, the Reverend Henry Francis Lyte preached his last sermon to the seafaring congregation to whom he had ministered for 23 years. His parish was in Brixham, on the wild Devon coast of England. At the time, Lyte was suffering from the prolonged effects of tuberculosis. He had to practically crawl up to the pulpit that day.

That evening, after the sermon, Reverend Lyte wrote down the words for a hymn he called *Abide With Me*. He based this on the text which tells the story of the risen Christ on the way to Emmaus and the disciples' statement, "Abide with us: for it is toward evening and the day is far spent."

> Abide with me: fast falls the eventide,
> The darkness deepens, Lord, with me abide;
> When other helpers fail and comforts flee,
> Help of the helpless, O abide with me!

Advised by his doctor to seek out the warmer climate of Italy, Lyte set out but never completed his journey, dying on arrival at the French port of Nice. His hymn remained relatively unknown until 1861, when a choirmaster and organist called William Monk wrote a new tune for it. Monk wrote it at a time of great personal sadness, when he had been inspired by a sunset.

For more than a century, the bells of Lyte's former church, All Saints in Lower Brixham, have rung out *Abide With Me* daily. The hymn has become known to millions worldwide. A favourite of Mahatma Gandhi, it was sung at his funeral. It was also sung at royal weddings. From 1927, for 70 years, it was chanted by 100,000 supporters at London's Wembley Stadium just before kick-off at the annual Football Association's Cup Final.

57. A dissatisfied draper's clerk

In 1840, a country-born man called George Williams was learning to become a draper. He had been a "careless, thoughtless, godless, swearing young fellow". But then he discovered the gospel of Jesus and became a devout Christian.

On his arrival in London, the young draper became very concerned with the plight of young men who, like him, had come to London for work. The lives of the 150,000 London shop assistants in 1841 were still little removed from those of slaves. Working twelve hours a day, six days a week, they had to sleep in crowded rooms over the shop, while their living conditions were severely lacking in hygiene, and their only recreation was drinking in saloons or visiting prostitutes.

George got together with several other drapers who were also Christians and they prayed for a solution. In 1844, they formed the Young Men's Christian Association (YMCA), affectionately known as "Ys".

By 1851, 24 Ys had been set up in Great Britain, and this was the year in which the Y arrived in both Montreal and Boston. Two years later a freed slave opened a Y for African-Americans. By 1854 there were 397 separate Ys in seven nations, with 30,369 members.

Williams was not memorable just for this. He was a crusader for improved working conditions such as shorter hours (a standard working day was fifteen or so hours), and, as he became a successful businessman, he gave away approximately two-thirds of his income. In his room hung a framed card illuminated with the words "God First".

Today, The World Alliance of YMCAs, headquartered in Geneva, Switzerland, has 30 million members in 110 countries. In the United States the YMCA serves 14 million people a year.

58. Glasgow businessman strives for unity

Scottish businessman John Henderson had not thought that he had a key role to play in the future of Christian unity.

The late 1830s was a disturbing time for the Christian church in Great Britain. Protestants were declaring themselves anti-Catholic, and Scottish Presbyterians were declaring themselves anti-Church of Scotland. Something had to be done.

A theologian called Thomas Chalmers had written a manuscript called *Essays on Christian Union*. But he needed a sponsor. That man was John Henderson of Glasgow. Publication of this little book led to a conference on Christian unity being held in Liverpool in October 1845. More than 200 leaders attended. The following year, an association of individual Christians of different denominations, calling itself The Evangelical Alliance, was formed in London, at a conference of over 900 clergymen and laymen from all parts of the world. They represented upwards of 50 sections of the Protestant Church. Their aim was to launch, in their own words, "a new thing in church history, a definite organisation for the expression of unity amongst Christian individuals belonging to different churches".

Today, 150 years after the London gathering, what has become the World Evangelical Alliance is a dynamic global structure for unity and action that embraces 160 million evangelicals in 111 countries.

59. Pastor's wife attacks slave trade

Although Harriet Beecher Stowe had managed to get several short stories published, since her marriage to a pastor she had

had her hands full, rearing five children in the first seven years of their marriage. The Beecher Stowes lived in Cincinnati, on the Ohio River. Ohio was a slave state, and Harriet was horrified to observe a black husband and wife, both slaves, being sold separately. She read about the sufferings of the slaves and the brutality of some of the slave-owners in newspapers and magazines. Her family shared her views and became active in hiding runaway slaves.

She decided to write a story for serialisation in the Washington anti-slavery weekly, the *National Era*. It was then printed in book form with the title *Uncle Tom's Cabin*. Following its publication, Harriet Beecher Stowe became a celebrity, speaking out against slavery in both Europe and America. She then wrote *A Key to Uncle Tom's Cabin* (1853), extensively documenting the realities on which the book was based, in order to refute critics who tried to argue that it was not authentic. *Uncle Tom's Cabin* was translated into over 25 languages and did much to hasten the American Civil War.

In 1862, when Mrs Beecher Stowe visited President Abraham Lincoln, legend claims that he greeted her as "the little lady who made this big war".

60. A modest composer

In 1844, the 20-year-old Anton Bruckner was scraping a living as a schoolmaster and organist in the villages surrounding his home in Ansfelden, Austria. He would wear peasant clothing, with baggy trousers and an oversized collar. He was very timid. But he had a burning ambition to devote his music to the glory of God. He began to write organ pieces.

By the time he was 40, Anton Bruckner felt ready to

compose his first real symphony. Yet he was so lacking in confidence that he called it Symphony No. 0.

Twenty years later, Bruckner had become admired throughout Europe as Austria's greatest composer of symphonies (nine of them in all), and of majestic choral works to the glory of God.

$61.$ An unsuitable profession

In 1854 Florence Nightingale took 38 women to Turkey to nurse wounded and sick British soldiers of the Crimean War. Until then, women had never been allowed to go out to the battlefront to tend to the suffering.

Moreover, while Florence's wealthy father had personally educated his daughters, he was totally opposed to the idea of Florence's becoming a nurse. Such a task was for working-class women only.

But since her teens Florence had felt herself to be called by God to some unnamed great cause. Encouraged by Elizabeth Blackwell, America's first qualified woman doctor, Florence completed her nurse's training despite her family's opposition.

Once in Turkey, Florence and her team courageously set about "cleaning up" the military hospitals, where lack of hygiene had killed more men than armed combat had. Many of the modern nursing systems and techniques we know today can be traced back to her.

$62.$ A nurse undeterred

In 1854, Mrs Mary Seacole, a qualified American nurse, arrived in England to offer her services to the British War

Office for the Crimean conflict. She was rejected. Not even Florence Nightingale would give her an interview. The problem was that Mary Seacole was a "negress".

Undeterred, she made her own way out to the Front and quickly set up her "British Hotel" near Balaclava, providing hot meals and other home comforts for the sick and wounded. "Mother Seacole" even ventured onto the battlefield to tend to the wounded and dying. News of her daring exploits travelled back to England, and Mary was hailed as a national heroine.

Upon returning to England in 1856, she was not reimbursed for her efforts and suffered bankruptcy. So she decided to publish her life story, *The Wonderful Adventures of Mrs Seacole in Many Lands*. Its success paid off her debts. Then Mrs Seacole faded from public attention for almost 100 years. In the 1970s Mrs Seacole was "rediscovered", and has become a symbol for black nurses, civil-rights groups and the women's liberation movement.

63. Clerk founds Chinese mission

One afternoon in 1849, a tired-eyed 17-year-old bank clerk called James Hudson Taylor went to the library of his Methodist-preacher father in search of something to read. Finally he picked up a gospel tract entitled "It is Finished". He came across the expression "The Finished Work of Christ". But then he reflected, "What is finished?" The answer seemed to fall into place and he received Christ as his Saviour.

His father had always been fascinated by China, and indeed when only four years old Hudson had once declared, "When I am a man I mean to be a missionary and go to China!"

He now resumed his vocation. Having studied the Chinese

language using a copy of Luke's gospel in the Mandarin dialect, and trained as a doctor at the London Hospital, Hudson Taylor travelled out to China in 1854. He was 21 years old.

During his 51 years of service there, Taylor's China Inland Mission established 20 mission stations, brought 849 missionaries to the field (968 by 1911), trained some 700 Chinese workers, raised four million dollars by faith, and developed a witnessing Chinese church of 125,000. It has been said at least 35,000 were his own converts and that he baptised some 50,000. His gift for inspiring people to give themselves and their possessions to Christ was amazing.

When he died, Christians carried his body to Chinkiang, where he was buried, alongside his wife, Maria, at the foot of green hills near the Yangtze River.

64. Former drunken delinquent evangelises Santals

In 1860, a young coppersmith who had taken to drink was serving a four-year prison sentence in a Norwegian jail. His name was Lars Olsen Skrefsrud. A girl he had known, Anna Olsum, remained faithful to Lars, visiting him in jail and bringing him books on religion. Following a talk with a visiting pastor, Lars decided to dedicate his life to serving Christ. Released from prison in 1861, aged 21, he went to the Gossner Missionary Society in Berlin. During his training, Lars lived almost entirely on bread, cheese and water. He prayed a great deal.

Two years later he left for India, where he joined a Baptist minister to work among the Santals of northern India. His girlfriend, Anna, joined him and they were married.

The Santals were an oppressed, illiterate tribe. Pastor Lars gave them a written language, translated the gospels into it, and wrote hymn-books and textbooks. He founded schools to teach them farming, animal husbandry, carpentry and other trades. When he died, there were about 20,000 baptised Santal Christians.

Lars Skrefsrud is buried in Santalistan and the Christian community he founded there continues to flourish 100 years later.

65. Canoeist and philanthropist

John MacGregor was a London barrister, who, through his extremely popular books and magazine articles from 1865 until 1892, practically invented the sport of canoeing. MacGregor had got the idea of canoeing for pleasure in his youth, from watching the Kamschatka tribes of North America, where his father was stationed.

During the 1860s, MacGregor paddled thousands of miles in his *Rob Roy* canoes: 1000 miles throughout the rivers, canals and lakes of Europe, then across Palestine and Egypt and the waters of Damascus; then to Scandinavia, Germany, the North Sea and the Baltic.

What is much less well known is that John MacGregor was a strong Christian philanthropist. Wherever he canoed, he always carried a number of copies of a pamphlet entitled *Muscular Christianity*, which he was always ready to hand out. He would never travel on the Sabbath, but lectured on his travels and gave many of the profits to charities such as the Royal National Lifeboat Institution and the Shipwrecked Mariners' Society. He was also one of the founders of the Shoe Black Brigade, which offered regular paid employment to children who made their living from cleaning boots and shoes. In the evenings, these children could attend lessons at the Ragged Schools.

MacGregor's influence was far-reaching, in both sport and missionary work. In Melbourne, for example, the Reverend Fairey had read about the voyages of the *Rob Roy* and acquired a similar canoe from England which he then used to preach the gospel to settlers on the rivers and coasts of the Australian colonies.

66. Steel baron promotes peace and education

By 1865, 30-year-old, Scottish-born Andrew Carnegie's business interests in the USA included iron- and steelworks, steamers on the Great Lakes, railroads and oil wells. Carnegie had become one of the wealthiest men in the world.

But Carnegie firmly believed that the only hope for the world was in the individual, society and the nations living by the teachings of Christ. He believed that all personal wealth beyond that required to supply the needs of one's family should be regarded as a trust fund to be administered for the benefit of the community.

By the time he died, in 1919, Carnegie had given away $350 million. One of his lifelong interests was the establishment of free public libraries to make a means of self-education available to everyone. There were only a few public libraries in the world when, in 1881, Carnegie began to promote his idea. He and his Corporation subsequently spent over $56 million on building 2,509 libraries throughout the English-speaking world. Similarly, his delight in organ music from childhood led to the donation of over 8,000 organs.

One of Carnegie's greatest longings was for peace among all nations. To this end, he established various trusts, the funding of which would go towards the study of the causes of war. Perhaps his greatest act towards furthering this objective was the construction of the one-million-pound Peace Palace in the Hague.

Even after his death, the Carnegie Corporation continued to maintain an interest in the improvement of library services for about 40 years. Other major programmes in the Corporation's early history included adult education, and education in the fine arts.

67. Mourning mother befriends the friendless

During the 1860s, Mr and Mrs George Butler must have suffered from their inability to prevent things from happening. George Butler was vice-principal of Cheltenham College, the expensive and fashionable public school for boys in Cheltenham, England. The US Civil War was raging across the Atlantic. Whilst other members of his staff favoured the Confederate whites, George and his wife, Josephine, were ostracised for being anti-slavery and pro-Union. Then, in 1863, they suffered a further setback when their six-year-old daughter fell to her death before their eyes.

They moved to Liverpool, where George obtained a post at the City College. As for Josephine, instead of staying at home like an obedient and grieving Victorian housewife, she began to care for friendless women, visiting the local workhouse and rescuing prostitutes from the streets. Despite shocked neighbours, she even accommodated some of them in her own home.

The Contagious Diseases Acts had set up government-policed brothels for soldiers and sailors, thereby virtually imprisoning young destitute women to a life of abuse.

Josephine Butler chose to lead a campaign for the repeal of these Acts, including the abolition of similar institutions in India. People were shocked that a middle-class teacher's wife should dare to speak in public about sexual matters. But in the end the Acts were repealed and Josephine extended her campaign into Europe and Scandinavia. She stopped only to nurse her husband, who had fallen seriously ill.

68. Songs from the heart

In the late 1860s, following the US Civil War, Tennessee's newly freed but impoverished black slaves found it difficult to get the education they so needed. When the Fisk Free Colored School opened in 1866, it operated on a shoestring. The school's treasurer, George L White, had been discharged from the Army because of broken health and was suffering as a result of having fought in several bloody battles, including Gettysburg. But he had a great love of music and began to give daily singing lessons to a handful of black students. Star of the group was a teenager called Ella Sheppard. As the Fisk School fell more deeply into debt, White decided to form a choir which would go on a fund-raising tour of Tennessee. It was a limited success.

But it was on this tour that White discovered how audiences warmed more to the plantation songs of sorrow and joy, which his singers had learned in their enslaved childhood, than to classical hymns. So he added more of these "spirituals" to the repertoire of his Jubilee Singers. After the statewide tour, White and his choir gave concerts in wealthy Brooklyn, New York. From there they crossed to Great Britain, where they were applauded by audiences of ten thousand, and even to Holland and Germany. And this despite

White's suffering from ill health and his choir from sheer exhaustion.

Over 125 years later, The Jubilee Singers are still inspiring people with the same spirituals that their ancestors sang on the cotton plantations . . .

69. Preacher invests in the poor

On his deathbed, William Booth's father, a nail-maker made bankrupt by new industrial methods, had told his poorly educated son to "make money". So young Booth had found work in a pawnbroker's shop. People desperately short of money would bring in their valuables in exchange for ready cash. If they failed to come back, the valuables became the property of the pawnbroker. This certainly made money. Booth was disturbed by this unfair situation, and moved by the plight of the people entering the shop. But how could he, a humble assistant, do anything about this? However, God had chosen William Booth.

At first he became a Methodist minister, preaching to a small street congregation in the slums of London. Thieves, prostitutes, gamblers and drunkards were among Booth's first converts to Christianity. His congregations were desperately poor. He preached hope and salvation. His aim was to lead them to Christ and link them to a church for continued spiritual guidance.

Even though Booth's followers were converted, churches did not accept them because of what they had been. However, Booth gave their lives direction in both a spiritual and a practical manner, and put them to work to save others who were like them. These people in turn preached and sang in the streets as a living testimony to the power of God.

In 1867, Booth had only ten full-time workers. By 1874, the numbers had grown to 1,000 volunteers and 42 evangelists. They served under the name "The Christian Mission" and Booth assumed the title of General Superintendent, although his followers called him "General". Known as the "Hallelujah Army", the converts spread out of the east end of London into neighbouring areas and then to other cities.

This international organisation is today known as The Salvation Army.

70. "My fellow lepers . . ."

In 1863, a 23-year-old Belgian missionary priest, Joseph Damien van Veuster, arrived in Hawaii. Soon afterwards, the islands were stricken by a severe epidemic of Hansen's disease, otherwise known as leprosy. This was dealt with largely by isolating those infected on the island of Molokai at Kalaupapa. Surrounded on three sides by the Pacific Ocean, and cut off from the rest of Molokai by 1600-foot (488m) sea cliffs, Kalaupapa was considered "safe". The infected were simply dumped there and left to fend for themselves. The crews of boats carrying them were afraid to land, so they simply came in close to the beach and forced the lepers to jump overboard. The outcasts lost their self-respect and took to drink and disordered sexuality.

In 1873, van Veuster (Father Damien) asked to be sent to Molokai Island to minister to the colony of 700 unfortunate victims. For the next 16 years he lived among the lepers. He began by organising Christian funerals and building coffins to give them greater dignity. He taught the people to grow crops, and assembled a choir. A new and larger chapel was built. Although doctors visited the island with supplies, they kept their distance. It was Father Damien who washed, anointed and bandaged their sores. He shared their life without fear – and without discretion or even common sense, so his critics said.

Father Damien always addressed his flock lovingly as "my dear brethren". But one Sunday in 1885, aged 45, the priest began with, "My fellow lepers, I am one of you now." After that he was an outcast even from his own church. His fellow priests would not use the chalice and vestments he used, and the missionary sisters would not receive communion from his hands.

He died of leprosy four years later.

71. War veteran saved from alcohol

A tramp walked into the Water Street Mission in New York. He was over six feet tall, and 60 years of age, but he looked 100. His dirty grey beard was a foot long, and his hair (of the same colour) hung a foot down his back. He had on an old, ragged overcoat, probably pulled out of some rubbish bin, and fastened with a nail. An old coat and waistcoat completed the look. His trousers could not be called a part of his outfit, as they were little more than holes with rags tied round them. He had no shirt on, and on his feet were pieces of rag tied up with string. "Old Colonel Bill" was a caricature of the man he had once been.

He was from one of Ohio's oldest and best families, from a wealthy, prosperous Christian home. After going through college, he had studied law. He entered the army at the outbreak of the Civil War, and served throughout that fearful struggle with credit, but was mustered out a colonel in an Illinois cavalry regiment, a confirmed drunkard. He tried to struggle against that deadly habit, which held him so securely in its grip, but it was useless. At last, when home, wife and children were gone, he became utterly discouraged. He gave up in despair and, on arriving in New York, took an assumed name.

Ultimately he came to be a street beggar. For over a quarter of a century he had been a confirmed drunkard. But then came the night of his conversion.

"Oh, Lord, if it is not too late," cried the old Colonel, "forgive and save this poor old sinner!" God heard the cry of his heart. He was gloriously saved. God restored his intellect. That which had been his greatest love and had almost ruined his life – strong drink – became his greatest hatred. He became an honoured and much loved Christian gentleman.

72. Ben Hur

Two former American Civil War officers were in a railroad train discussing the life of Christ. Colonel Robert Ingersoll, well known for his atheism, suggested to his friend, General Lew Wallace, that an interesting fiction romance could be written about the life of Christ.

"Tear down the prevailing sentiment about his divinity, and paint him as a man, a man among men."

Wallace took up the challenge and went off researching in the leading libraries of America and Europe. But then, in the process of constructing the life of Christ, Lew Wallace found himself faced with the greatest life ever lived on earth. While writing the second chapter of his book, he suddenly found himself on his knees, crying out, "My Lord and my God!"

The book he wrote, entitled *Ben-Hur: A Tale of the Christ*, was first published in November 1880. It immediately became the bestselling novel of the 19th century, and for decades was outsold only by the Bible itself. It was translated into every major language of the world and has never been out of print. The Wallace Museum library in Crawfordsville, Indiana currently contains 92 different editions of the book, but it is estimated that there are four times that number. *Ben-Hur* has twice formed the subject of a spectacular film.

73. Hindu discovers Jesus Christ

Mary Ramabai was born in western India. She was raised in a very orthodox Hindu family steeped in Sanskrit, one of the oldest languages in the world. Indeed, her father was a Sanskrit scholar who believed in educating women. His daughter would become fluent in seven languages, with knowledge of several others.

After a stay in England, Mary Ramabai discovered Jesus Christ. In 1882, aged 24, she established the Arya Mahila Samaj for the cause of furthering women's Christian-based education in Pune (Poona) and other parts of western India. She campaigned in the USA to raise funds for residential schools for widows in India. She helped to set up homes for orphans. She opposed the traditions of caste and child marriage in her country. She translated the Bible into Marathi, her mother tongue.

Mary Ramabai became the first woman to be awarded the title "Pandita" or "Saraswati" by Sanskrit scholars at Calcutta University. She died in 1922.

74. Silk merchant preaches salvation

During the late 1860s, despite spinal weakness, Wilson Carlile had used his fluent French, Italian and German to build up a prosperous trade in the silk industry. Then, in 1873, he was ruined in a slump.

Following a serious illness, Wilson Carlile became a Christian and an Anglican. When American evangelist Ira Sankey was touring England, Carlile acted as his organist. In 1881 he was ordained curate in a London parish.

Almost immediately, Carlile realised that there was a serious lack of contact between the church and the working classes. He began preaching outdoors. In 1882, he resigned his curacy and founded the Church Army.

75. Banker's son captivated by the Bible

Paul Claudel had been brought up as a non-believer in a gentrified farming family in the French département of Aisne. His father, Louis-Prosper, dealt in mortgages and bank transactions. But then, on Christmas Day, 25th December 1886, the 18-year-old Claudel went into the Notre Dame Cathedral in Paris. There, as he later recounted, he heard, as from a voice above, "There is a God".

In the years that followed, the Bible became the centre of Claudel's world and his inspiration. Although a widely travelled diplomat, Claudel became renowned as a playwright, poet and essayist, whose work showed great spiritual intensity. Claudel became a leading figure in the revival movement for French Catholics during the early part of the 20th century.

76. A lieutenant seeks God

Viscount Charles de Foucauld was born in Strasbourg, France in the 19th century. In his youth he became an atheist, and as a young lieutenant in the 1870s, he enjoyed a wild and unorthodox life. One day he disguised himself as a tramp and went begging for bread in a village. In 1880, his regiment, the 4th Hussars, was sent to Algeria and he continued to show a total lack of discipline and engage in "notorious conduct". He took part in the eight-month campaign to suppress the revolt of Bou-Amama, during which time the Arabs had a profound effect on him, so deep in fact that he went on leave, learned Arabic and Hebrew, and made a long-term reconnaissance expedition into Morocco.

Returning to Paris to write up his expedition, de Foucauld began his spiritual voyage. One day he entered a church and expressed this prayer: *"Mon Dieu, si Vous existez, faites que je Vous connaisse"* (God, if you exist, make yourself known to me). At the end of October 1886, at the Church of Saint Augustine, de Foucauld made his first confession and received his first Holy Communion.

In the years to come he became a Trappist monk in France and Syria, a hermit in Nazareth, a garrison priest at Beni-Abbès, Algeria, and a nomadic hermit among the Tuareg around Tamanrasset, where he was eventually murdered. Brother Charles of Jesus felt called to imitate Christ by leading a life of personal poverty in small contemplative communities financed solely by their own manual labour. His ideals survived in the founding of the Little Brothers (1933) and Little Sisters (1939) of Jesus, now active worldwide.

77. Champion cricketer goes to China

In the 1880s, missionary fervour spread among undergraduates at Cambridge University, England. The Cambridge Seven were touring the big cities of Great Britain, witnessing as to how and why they were joining Hudson Taylor's China Inland Mission to spread the gospel. At the centre of this group was perhaps the least likely young man to have made such a decision.

From an upper-class family, Charles Studd had become a national star in the highly popular British game of cricket. Whilst an undergraduate at Trinity College, Cambridge, Studd had played brilliant cricket for his university for four consecutive years and was the first undergraduate ever to play in a test match against the Australians.

Then he went to hear the fervent preaching of two visiting American evangelists, Dwight Moody and Ira Sankey. This changed Charles Studd's life. He publicly announced his decision to abandon cricket to become a missionary. Six other Cambridge undergraduates followed Studd's example, one of them a promising lieutenant in the Royal Artillery.

The influence of the Cambridge Seven was dynamic. At a meeting at Exeter Hall, London in 1885, 40 other Cambridge graduates publicly announced their decision to become missionaries.

Out in China, the Cambridge Seven were to meet with almost insurmountable challenges, but they continued as missionaries as long as their health remained strong. Charles Studd eventually moved to Africa where he helped to start the Worldwide Evangelization Crusade, now known as WEC International.

78. Unlikely missionary

Waswa Munubi was a Muslim soldier under orders to murder the Christians in his native Uganda in Africa. He was also a drug addict, regularly smoking hemp. But during his military service he deserted and fled to Ankole, where he joined the Anglican Mission. He became a Christian, and in 1895 was baptised as "Apolo Kivebulaya".

Soon afterwards, when the Anglican Church was seeking a missionary to go to Boga in the African Congo, Apolo offered to go. Taking only his Bible and his hoe, he walked over the rugged Rwenzori Mountains, crossed a river, and travelled for 50 miles through the dense forest of Boga.

Despite resistance from the polygamous, sorcery-dominated and alcohol-drinking tribe, who attempted to starve him out, Apolo did not give up. Eventually the tribe and their chief, Tabaro, became Christians.

In 1900 Apolo was ordained and made Rural Dean of Toro.

Apolo declared the year 1921 "the Year of the Gospel". He took the gospel to the inhabitants of the forest: the Walese, the Wanyali, and the Wambuti (the latter are pygmies). He said, "Christ appeared before me as a man. It was like seeing a man who was my brother. He said to me: 'Go, preach in the forest, because I am with you. I am who I am – this is my Name.'" Apolo went amongst these peoples as a friend, eating their food and sleeping in their mud huts. He baptised pygmies for the first time in 1932.

He is remembered for building several churches in Mboga and translating Matthew's gospel into Runyoro. He also translated a book for the pygmies in the neighbouring forest area which contained the Lord's Prayer, the Commandments and hymns.

79. Bibles for all

In September 1898, John Nicholson, a travelling salesman, attempted to check into the Central House Hotel in Boscobel, Wisconsin. As the hotel was hosting a lumbermen's convention, no single rooms were available. The hotel manager asked Nicholson to share a room with another salesman, Samuel Hill. That evening, in Room 19, the two men discovered that they were both Christians. Having prayed together and read the Bible, they discussed the need for a Christian commercial travellers' association.

Nothing more might have happened. But then a chance meeting the following May rekindled the idea. On 1st July 1899, the two salesmen, joined by a third, William Knights, met in Janesville and founded an association which they called The Gideons. The name comes from the Old Testament book of Judges, and refers to a man who was willing to do whatever God asked of him.

At the start, the Gideons had the idea of presenting every hotel manager with a Bible for his front desk. Then, in 1907, this progressed to a Bible for each hotel bedroom in the USA. Within 20 years of the first placement, the association had distributed 1 million Bibles.

To date, the Gideons have given away 870 million Bibles and New Testaments. The movement has 140,000 members, mostly volunteers, in 172 countries. This averages one million books every eight days, or 86 per minute. Evangelical churches of many denominations financially support the Gideons' work of distributing Bibles, not only to hotels but also to hospitals, prisons, primary schools, universities and military bases.

80. God's money or mine?

In the early 1900s, RG LeTourneau was earning his living by shovelling sand and dirt at an ironworks in Portland, Oregon, USA. He was little interested in the ways of God, even though his parents were fervent Christians.

Moving to California, LeTourneau worked at almost 40 different jobs. He married a girl twelve years younger than he was and they lost their first child in infancy. Following this, he badly injured his neck during a stock-car race. By 31 he was $5,000 in debt. It was then that he prayed to God for help.

A kind bank manager agreed to extend a loan enabling LeTourneau to buy a tractor and a scraper in order to go into the earth-moving business. In the years that followed, he became an extremely successful engineering inventor and industrialist, specialising in massive earth-transporters, bridge-builders, huge portable offshore drilling rigs and the electric wheel. LeTourneau built many of the machines that were used during the Allied Invasion to liberate Europe in 1944/45.

But for many years, this same man lived on only 10% of his income, with the rest going towards bringing the gospel, education and medical aid to thousands in Liberia, West Africa and Peru, South America, and also towards establishing a university in Texas. "The question is not how much of my money I give to God, but rather how much of God's money I keep for myself," he said.

81. Mission on Azusa Street

1906: Houston, Texas: A black, 20-year-old, one-eyed, former railroad porter and waiter called William J Seymour, son of former slaves, sat in the hallway of a religious meeting. Texas law still forbade blacks to sit in classrooms with whites.

But three years later the word spread that Seymour was "speaking in tongues" at a house in Los Angeles. Crowds began to gather. Moving to an abandoned church on Azusa Street, Seymour and a small team of willing black helpers set up the "Apostolic Faith Mission". Hundreds began to flock there to witness preaching in tongues, trances and dancing. There was no order of service, since "the Holy Ghost was in control". Other Pentecostal churches grew up, while some 50,000 people regularly read Seymour's publication *The Apostolic Faith.*

By the year 2000, the spiritual heirs of Seymour, the Pentecostals and Charismatics, numbered over 500 million adherents, making it the second largest family of Christians in the world. Today, practically all Pentecostal and Charismatic movements can trace their roots directly or indirectly to the humble mission on Azusa Street and its pastor.

82. A musicologist with a passion to help Africa

By the time he had reached 30, Albert Schweitzer, a native of Alsace on the Franco-German border, had achieved international renown as a brilliant musicologist, theologian and accomplished organist. His books on these three subjects were recognised as important contributions to the history of music, the improvement of organ design, and a more profound and challenging understanding of the lives of Jesus Christ and St Paul. He might have spent the rest of his life writing and giving organ recitals.

But then one day Schweitzer came upon a report of the Paris Missionary Society and an article headed *The Needs of the Congo Mission*. He realised that there was other work to do. In 1913, having studied tropical medicine, Dr Schweitzer abandoned his comfortable life in Strasbourg and travelled out to Lambaréné, a deserted mission station in French Equatorial Africa (Gabon). There, helped by his wife, he set up a hospital to fight leprosy and sleeping sickness. Other than returning to Europe to raise funds for his hospital by giving organ recitals and lectures, Dr Schweitzer remaining working at his self-built hospital until his death, aged 90.

83. A champagne dealer

In 1915 a torpedo launched from a German U-boat sank the British ocean liner *Lusitania* as she neared the end of an east-bound transatlantic crossing. Among those few survivors who spent seven hours in a collapsible boat was a wealthy New York wine merchant called George Kessler. In New York, Kessler had come to be known as "the champagne king", importing and selling on the best wines to wealthy clients.

While fellow survivors were washed overboard, Kessler clung on, resolving that if he lived he would devote his energy and resources to helping war victims.

While in hospital, Kessler met the blind newspaper publisher Sir Arthur Pearson, who told him about St Dunstan's, a centre he had started up to help men blinded in the war.

Six months after his shipwreck, Kessler and his wife organised the Permanent Blind Relief War Fund on both sides of the

Atlantic. Schools and workshops were set up. A braille printing press eventually printed 5 million pages of books, distributed to 40 libraries.

Today the American Foundation for the Overseas Blind (AFOB) is a dynamic worldwide organisation.

84. The electronic church

By 1910, a 30-year-old former pastor called Paul Rader was working in the public relations department of an oil company. He considered his father's Methodist Christianity a bygone relic of his immature youth.

But one evening Rader was walking near Times Square in New York City when God spoke to him through a neon-illuminated sign. He rented a room nearby and fell on his face before the Lord, and his life was changed. He left his business and went back into the ministry.

Rader had been working as pastor at several Tabernacle churches when in June 1922 he received an extraordinary opportunity. William "Big Bill" Thompson, eccentric mayor of gangster-ruled Chicago, had set up a radio station on the roof of the city hall. Its call sign was "WBU". Lacking programme material, Mayor Thompson issued a general call for volunteers. He hoped that professional entertainers would respond but they were suspicious of radio and refused. The least likely, Paul Rader, accepted. He brought along his musicians, went up on the roof and produced a typical evangelistic service on the air. From that first broadcast, Rader's folksy speaking style became a big hit. In time, his tabernacle became known as "The Church that Blesses Thousands".

Just six months later, at the fledgling British Broadcasting

Company in London, call sign 2LO, the Reverend J Mayo gave the first ever religious address.

The Electronic Church was born.

85. The rights of the child

Eglantyne Jebb was born into a well-to-do country family in Shropshire, England in 1876. As a child she was something of a tomboy, playing at soldiers and riding horses. She remained headstrong, even at university.

Attempting to work as a teacher in a primary school for slum children, Jebb felt herself to be a failure. She also began to suffer from severe fatigue because of thyroid problems. Then, in 1900, she became a committed Christian. It was a pivotal moment in her life.

Having seen the horrors of war, and the sufferings of child refugees, Eglantyne Jebb and her sister formed the Save the Children Fund for an initial contribution of £10. Before long a donation of £10,000 arrived from British miners to help the starving children in Vienna. Soon afterwards, Save the Children associations were also founded in Sweden, Australia and Canada.

In February 1923, Eglantyne Jebb went to Geneva. On a Sunday afternoon, sitting on the side of Mount Saleve, she wrote down the first version of the Rights of the Child. The following year, its five clauses were adopted by the League of Nations. By 1924 the International Save the Children Union had 20 members, including: the UK, Sweden, Switzerland, Germany, Austria, Hungary, Ireland, Italy, Latvia, Norway, Romania, Yugoslavia, Turkey and Uruguay.

By 1998 the United Nations Convention on the Rights of the Child had been ratified by all but two countries on earth.

86. Athlete missionary

Eric Liddell was born in January 1902 in Tientsin, northern China, the son of missionaries. In 1943 he was working as a missionary there when he was sent to a Japanese prisoner-of-war camp, where he died two years later. Like so many others, Eric Liddell might never have left the mission field.

But in his youth, Liddell had not only gained a BSc degree in pure science at Edinburgh University, he was also a good rugby player and an even better athlete. In 1924 Liddell went to the Olympic Games, held in Paris, to compete in the 100-metre sprint. When he learned that the heats were to be run on a Sunday, rather than dishonour the Lord by running on the Sabbath he gave up his chance and switched to the 400 metres. Arms thrashing, head bobbing and tilted, Liddell ran to victory, five metres ahead of the silver medallist. "The Flying Scotsman" had achieved a gold medal and a world record, 47.6 seconds.

After the Olympic Games, Eric Liddell returned to northern China to resume his work for the Lord.

87. Blind and deaf leader

Helen Keller from Alabama was only 19 months old when she contracted meningitis, which robbed her of both her sight and her hearing. When she was almost seven years old, her parents engaged Anne Mansfield Sullivan to be her tutor. With dedication, patience, courage and love, Miss Sullivan was able to bring out and help develop the child's enormous intelligence. Helen Keller quickly learned to read and write. By the age of ten she had begun to speak. At the age of 20, she entered Radcliffe College, with Miss Sullivan at her side to spell textbooks – letter by letter – into her hand. Four years later, Radcliffe awarded Helen Keller a BA degree *magna cum laude*.

From 1900 until her death in 1968, Helen Keller devoted her life and energies to helping blind and deaf people. In 1928 she persuaded the leaders of several Christian denominations to develop an interdenominational ministry that would bring spiritual guidance and religious literature to deaf and blind persons. Helen decided to name the new society after John Milton, the great English writer and poet of the 17th century (1608–1675). John Milton was chosen because of his strong Christian faith and because he was one who, after losing his eyesight, did not give up but continued to write and went on to create prose, volume after volume of poetry and a number of hymns. John Milton lost his sight soon after he turned 40, and was blind when he wrote his epic poem *Paradise Lost* which reflects the inner soul's "Celestial Light" to "see and tell of things invisible to mortal sight".

Helen Keller founded the John Milton Society for the Blind in New York. She became its first president and remained Honorary President until her death in 1968.

88. Writer admits God is God

His mother's death in 1908 from cancer when CS "Jack" Lewis had been only nine years old, coupled with other experiences, caused this well-read young Englishman to reject Christianity and become an avowed atheist. From 1924, while Lewis was teaching English at Oxford University, he began to read books and have discussions with colleagues – such as JRR Tolkien – during which his atheism was severely challenged. So much so that, in 1929, "Jack" Lewis admitted "that God was God, and knelt and prayed".

During the next 30 years, Lewis was to write 25 works on Christianity, including *The Screwtape Letters* (1942) and *The Chronicles of Narnia* (1950–1956). While his colleagues at Oxford University did not appreciate Lewis's evangelistic approach, Cambridge University was prepared to honour him, and in 1955 he became Professor of Medieval and Renaissance English. That year his autobiography *Surprised by Joy* described his conversion to Christianity.

89. Lawyer sifts the evidence

His real name was Albert Henry Ross. Although he had obtained a law degree, he later became a journalist and advertising executive. In the late 1890s, as a young man influenced by those thinkers of the period who would "prove" the non-existence of Jesus Christ, he set about writing a short paper entitled Jesus – the Last Phase. He would prove that the story of Christ's resurrection was only a myth.

> I wanted to take this last phase of the life of Jesus, with all its quick and pulsating drama, its sharp, clear-cut background of antiquity, and its tremendous psychological and human interest – and strip it of its overgrowth of primitive beliefs and dogmatic suppositions, and to see this supremely great Person as He really was.

Using his legal training, Ross began rigidly to sift the evidence, and admitted nothing which did not meet the criteria for a law court today. However, while he was doing his research, a remarkable thing happened. The case was not nearly as easy as he had supposed. He found that the evidence for the resurrection was so overwhelming that he was forced to accept it. He became a believer.

Under the pseudonym of Frank Morison, his book *Who Moved the Stone?* was first published in 1930. Its first chapter is called "The Book that Refused to be Written".

Morison's book became a bestseller and was printed in edition after edition, even after the author's death in 1983. It is still in print today.

90. A strategy for summer camps

In 1917, a 19-year-old insurance clerk called Eric Nash was commuting by train from London to his home in Maidenhead when God spoke to him.

Instead of becoming a missionary to the poor and needy, Nash thought up a least likely idea. The educational system in the British Isles had, and still has, a series of expensive, élite private schools, paradoxically known as public schools. Many pupils sent to these schools later go on to hold important and responsible posts in society. Nash realised that, if these teenagers understood and accepted the message of Christ, they would organise and delegate in a more considerate way.

So it was that from 1930, "Bash", as he came to be affectionately known, began to organise summer camps for groups of public-school boys. During the next ten years, a regular 100–200 schoolboys from 22 public schools would come together at venues on England's south coast. On the outbreak of World War II, and for the next three decades, Bash's camps were held at a little village called Iwerne Minster in Dorset, with numbers growing to over 300 per year. In time, there were also camps for public schoolgirls.

Many of Bash's campers went on to become archbishops, bishops and influential Christian leaders throughout the world.

91. Save the Children

By 1932, the bleakest year of the Depression in the United States, Clarke J Calvitt, a Presbyterian minister, veteran promoter of relief for peoples displaced by the ravages of World War I, and a gifted publicist and fund-raiser, again turned his concern for children in need into action. With Dr Nagle and another colleague, Dr John Voris, he co-founded Save the Children, US, inspired by the work of Eglantyne Jebb. Their goal was to aid children in Harlan County, Kentucky, one of the most impoverished regions of the country.

It all began in one single room in the Presbyterian Building at 156 Fifth Avenue, New York City.

After a two-month study of the health and sanitary situation in Harlan County, Kentucky, a local committee was established. In the spring of 1932, under the leadership of John Voris, the founding Executive Director, two surveys were conducted concerning children's needs. At its summer meeting that year, the board authorised the first Save the Children field project, a country health unit. A new form of sponsorship emerged from Save the Children's European experience: American "godparents" donated $30 a year to provide clothing and other necessities to a particular child. This approach was the model for the Save the Children child-sponsorship programmes that continue today.

92. Parlourmaid leads children to safety

Gladys Aylward had left school aged fourteen to become a parlourmaid in fashionable London. After attending a religious revival meeting, she had a burning ambition to travel to

China as a missionary. When she joined the China Mission Centre in 1930, this 28-year-old had never travelled further than the Isle of Wight, half-an-hour's pleasureboat trip from the south coast of England. Unable to pass the Mission's qualifying exam, Gladys returned to being a parlourmaid, saving up every penny to travel to the other side of the world by train and boat.

On her arrival, based at Yangcheng, Gladys and an ageing Scottish missionary, Mrs Lawson, ran their outpost, the Inn of the Sixth Happiness, to welcome travellers and tell them about Christ. From here, in 1938, Gladys made a trek across the mountains, leading over 100 orphans to safety, after the war with Japan had brought fighting to that area. Political upheavals and ill health obliged her to return to England, where a biography of her entitled *Small Woman* was later turned into a successful film, *Inn of the Sixth Happiness*. Gladys Aylward spent the rest of her life looking after refugees and orphans in Hong Kong and Taiwan.

93. Under threat

During World War I, he had served as a naval lieutenant, then as a commander in the ruthless "wolf pack" fleet of German submarines (or U-Boote) in the Kaiser's Navy. He had even been decorated.

But, by 1924, Martin Niemöller had become a pastor in the Lutheran Church.

In 1933 Hitler's Third Reich promulgated a "sterilisation" programme against both the Jews and the Christians. During the next years, thousands of priests, nuns and lay readers were arrested.

While the fearful in the Lutheran Church formed "the new

German Church", rejecting the Old Testament and the Jews, and swearing allegiance to Nazism, Pastor Niemöller formed a resistance movement called "The Confessing Church".

Among those who joined Niemöller was a German theologian and pastor by the name of Dietrich Bonhoeffer, who had been welcoming Christian and Jewish refugees from Nazi-dominated Germany to the safety of his parish in London, England. Pastor Bonhoeffer might well have stayed in London.

But then, in 1935, he decided to return to Germany, where the Confessing Church was under increasing pressure from the Gestapo. Whenever members of this church were publicly identified, they were sent off to the Eastern Front and almost certain death.

When this "underground" Christian community was closed down in 1937, Niemöller and Bonhoeffer joined the German Resistance. With others, the two pastors reasoned that, as Hitler was the anti-Christ, he should be assassinated. The attempt failed and the Christian assassins were arrested. Bonhoeffer was sent from an ordinary prison to a Gestapo prison to Buchenwald Concentration Camp, and finally to the Flossenburg Camp where he was hanged in April 1945.

The SS doctor who witnessed Bonhoeffer's death later recalled, "I have hardly ever seen a man die so entirely submissive to the will of God."

Niemöller was transferred to the infamous Dachau Concentration Camp – and survived. When the war was over, he emerged from his years of detention a towering symbol of the church's struggle. In his travels to America, Niemöller addressed over 200 audiences.

94. A POW composer

In 1941, a unique, one-hour concert was given, in sub-zero temperatures, to the 5,000 inmates and guards of the Stalag VIIIA prison camp at Görlitz in Nazi-occupied Silesia. The music had been composed in the camp by one of the inmates, a 33-year-old French soldier by the name of Olivier Messiaen. Based on the Book of Revelation, the eight movements of *Le Quatuor pour la fin du temps* had been orchestrated for the only instruments available at the camp: clarinet, piano, violin and cello.

Instead of the music having a traditional, classical structure, it was based on previous studies of Indian and Greek music, Gregorian chant and birdsongs. Messiaen, a devout Christian, believed birdsong to be symbolic of the angels. He had developed his hypnotic, meditative style to create "a music for eternity".

From the end of the war until his death in 1992, Messiaen often wrote music to interpret the life of Christ, such as *Ascension*, *La Transfiguration* and *Saint François d'Assise*.

"This is the most important aspect of my music," he once said. "Perhaps the only one I shall not be ashamed of in the hour of death."

95. Former refugee helps refugees

When Georges Pire was four years old, he and his family fled from Belgium before the advancing troops in 1914, spending four years in France before returning to find their home a charred ruin.

By 1937, the Reverend "Henri Dominique" Pire, aged 27,

was teaching sociology and moral philosophy at the Dominican Monastery of La Sarte in Huy, Belgium. There he might have remained as a teacher. But the following year he founded a service for mutual family aid and open-air camps for children. During World War II, these camps became missions that fed thousands of Belgian and French children.

During the war, Father Pire became chaplain to the Resistance movement, helping in the underground escape system for downed Allied airmen. For his services, this man of peace was awarded several military medals.

The 1950s saw Father Pire devoting his entire energies to helping refugees. Eighteen thousand refugee families were sponsored and received aid parcels. Four homes for the aged were set up. Seven villages, each for about 150 homeless, were constructed on the outskirts of German cities. Funds were raised by a crusade called "Europe of the Heart". Following his being awarded the Nobel Peace Prize in 1959, Father Pire expanded this to "The Heart Open to the World", its objective: international fraternity. In 1960, Father Pire founded the University of Peace at Huy, with the World Friendships Agency to help refugee families in Africa and Asia. Before his death in 1969, the unrelenting Belgian-born priest had been setting up refugee family self-help programmes in Pakistan.

96. Capturing voices

In 1930, Joy Ridderhof went with the Friends Mission Board to Honduras, her testing ground for the next six years. She based her ministry around the outlying town of Marcala and its neighbouring villages. She endured many sacrifices, both material and physical. Debilitating bouts of flu, malaria and smallpox took their toll. "In 1936, I returned from Honduras ill in body," recounted Joy, "disqualified for future missionary service and without financial support. It was a dark picture indeed."

Living in a tiny Los Angeles apartment, Joy continued to pray for the people she had left behind. Then an idea came to her. She remembered the gramophone records played in the villages, blaring out songs in English and Spanish. If she could make a record including messages from the gospel and Christian songs in Spanish, then it could do what she no longer could.

In 1939, the first record was made and sent to missionaries who would take it into the mountain areas. The response was terrific and soon requests were coming in from many parts of the Spanish-speaking world. Then one day a request came from missionaries to the Navajo Indians. A bilingual Navajo was willing to travel to Los Angeles to record the messages if Joy was willing to help. Joy realised that to begin recording in even one new language would be the start of something bigger than she had ever dreamed.

Soon Joy was convinced that this was from God. "Lord, I'll make recordings in as many languages as you want me to," she responded. She called her growing enterprise "Gospel Recordings". Requests from missionaries took her to the Eskimos of Alaska and the Mazahua Indians of Mexico. Others soon joined her in this exciting work.

When Joy died in 1984, Gospel Recordings had already captured the good news in over 4,000 languages in every country, including unreached preliterate groups of less than 10,000. GR currently has 60 recording operators. Thirty distribution centres are scattered across the globe, in places such as Mexico, India and Nigeria.

97. Two novels

Lloyd C Douglas, Minister of the Congregational Church in Ann Arbor, Michigan, fully understood the concept of "the least likely" when he wrote his novels about religious and moral themes. The manuscript of his first book, entitled *Magnificent Obsession*, had already been rejected by two major American publishers when a small religious publishing firm accepted it. It was to sell 3 million copies, which in the 1940s made it a bestseller.

The story is about Bobby Merrick, a neurosurgeon who is given the secret journal of his mentor, which contains the magic formula for success. The journal is written in code, which is miraculously deciphered by the young neurosurgeon. He learns of a "particular investment of himself as a high altruism". Dr Merrick finds that fulfilment is best achieved by providing service for others in secret. He experiences the joy of doing wonderful things for people in need. He requires secrecy, and suggests, if possible, that the good deed be passed on to someone else in need. *Magnificent Obsession* was twice adapted for the screen.

Douglas' novel *The Robe*, published in 1942, is even more vivid. The protagonist is a young Roman soldier, Marcellus, the son of Marcus Lucan Gallio, a senator. As punishment for ridiculing a speech by a close friend of Emperor Tiberius, Marcellus is sent to an outpost of the Empire. There he is ordered to crucify a Galilean named Jesus. To get through the awful crucifixion, the soldiers get drunk and play dice for Christ's robe. Marcellus wins. When he puts it on, something comes over him. He becomes haunted by the death of Jesus. Marcellus then starts his quest to find the truth about Jesus. He becomes a convert and a martyr to the new religion in Rome's Coliseum.

The Robe was made into a lavish Technicolor film in 1953. It received five Academy Award nominations and won two.

98. Tortured pianist forgives

At 18 years old, Maïti Girtanner looked likely to become a brilliant concert pianist. In June 1940, the Nazis invaded her native country, France. Living alongside the River Vienne, near Poitiers, one side of which was occupied and the other a free zone, Maïti began to smuggle escapees to freedom simply by rowing them across, hidden in the bottom of her boat.

She and some friends set up a Resistance cell and continued this for three years. To keep up a cover, Maïti gave piano recitals to the billeted Nazi officers.

But then in 1943 she was detected by Gestapo agents. They sent her to a "reprisal camp" for "terrorists" such as herself. Here a young doctor called "Leo" proceeded to "experimentally" torture her to the point of destroying her central nervous system.

While waiting to die, Maïti and the other prisoners shared Jesus' love and forgiveness, often within earshot of Leo.

Maïti survived, thanks to the Red Cross. She could never play the piano again and remained in daily pain. In 1984, Leo, living in his native Austria, was told he had a terminal illness. Afraid, he decided that the only person who might help him was his former victim.

He rediscovered her in France. She received him and they spent time together. He asked her forgiveness, and she pardoned him through the love of Jesus. He died a Christian, at peace.

99. A prisoner of war

Early in 1942, Colonel Jimmy Doolittle of the United States Army Air Corps won approval for a daring secret mission: to bomb Tokyo. On 18th April, Doolittle launched 16 medium bombers from the deck of an aircraft carrier off the coast of Japan. The bombers, however, would not be able to return to the carrier. Instead, the crews would have to crash-land or parachute into occupied China, and do their best to avoid capture.

Corporal Jacob DeShazer was a crew member on the last bomber to take off. His plane bombed some oil tanks and an industrial building, then headed for China. It was hit by enemy anti-aircraft bullets and he was forced to bail out. DeShazer survived the parachute jump but was soon captured and imprisoned. He was to endure torture, abuse and neglect at the hands of the Japanese for 40 months. During this time, he saw two of his companions shot by a firing squad, and another die from slow starvation. He could hardly contain his rage at his captors, and thought at times that he would go crazy.

During the long months of imprisonment, he pondered the question of why the Japanese hated him and why he hated them. In peacetime he had been an atheist, but then he began to recall some of the things he had heard about Christianity.

Boldly he asked his jailers if they could get him a Bible. At first they laughed loudly, grew ugly, and warned him to stop making a nuisance of himself. But he kept asking. A year-and-a-half later, in May 1944, a guard finally brought him a Bible. He flung it at him and said, "Three weeks you have. Three weeks and then I take away."

DeShazer immersed himself in it. The words seemed to come alive. His rage and hatred for the Japanese began to fade as his heart melted. Obeying the Lord's command to love his enemies, he forced himself to return kindness for their brutality.

True to his word, after three weeks the guard took the Bible away. DeShazer never saw it again. Later he was released from Japanese captivity and returned home. In 1948, DeShazer, along with his wife and infant son, went to Japan, this time as missionaries.

100. Love triumphs in concentration camp

In peacetime, the Ten Boom family had run a small, respectable, watch-making business in Haarlem, in the Netherlands. But, following the Nazi occupation of that country, their Christian faith led them to hide Jews, students and "underground" Resistance workers in their home. With the network they set up, they saved an estimated 80 Jews, not to mention many others.

But they were betrayed in February 1944, arrested by the Gestapo and sent to prison camps. Sisters Corrie and Betsie Ten Boom, both in their fifties, ended up in Barracks 28 at the notorious Ravensbrück Concentration Camp near Berlin. But even there they shared Jesus' love with other inmates.

Although Betsie did not survive, Corrie returned home to Haarlem. During the next four decades she established a worldwide ministry that took her to 64 countries, where she testified to Jesus' love and forgiveness. Her book *The Hiding Place* became a bestseller and she made five films.

Corrie Ten Boom died on her 91st birthday.

101. Flying missionary

Betty Green had dropped out of her nursing studies at the University of Washington. She was interested only in flying, and her hometown of Seattle, with the impressive Boeing factory nearby, seemed just the place to be.

But then one day an elderly Christian woman made an unlikely suggestion to the would-be flyer: that she combine her flying with missionary work. Flying could save missionaries invaluable time. During World War II, Betty became a WASP (Women's Air Force Service Pilot), ferrying many kinds of plane from factory to airfield. She also became a high-altitude test pilot.

In 1945, a US Navy pilot called Jim Thruxton read a magazine article by Betty about using planes to spread the gospel. They got together. On May 1945, the Christian Airmen's Missionary Fellowship was formed with USAF, RAF and RAAF pilots. Later its name was changed to the Mission Aviation Fellowship (MAF).

In 1946 Betty flew the Fellowship's first mission, taking a red Waco biplane to Mexico to help Wycliffe Bible Translators in their jungle training camp. By 1962 Betty had flown more than 4,800 hours, bringing medical supplies and food to missionaries, ferrying sick and injured people to hospitals, and carrying missionary children to their schools or to be with their parents for vacations. She served in Mexico, Peru, Africa and Indonesia. By the time of her death in 1997, hundreds of MAF pilots were operating and maintaining over 145 aircraft, flying in and out of some 4,000 airstrips around the world.

102. Missionary on the streets

In 1937, 27-year-old Sister Teresa, born Agnes Gonxha Bojaxhiu in Albania, was principal of a secondary school for middle-class Bengali girls in the centre of Calcutta, and Mother Superior of a diocesan order of Indian nuns, the

Daughters of St Anne, teachers in Calcutta's secondary schools. Sister Teresa taught history and geography in one of the city's most attractive neighbourhoods.

However, close by was one of Calcutta's great slums, and Sister Teresa became more and more concerned for the poor. In 1948, she came across a half-dead woman lying in front of a Calcutta hospital. She stayed with the woman until she died. Soon afterwards, with the consent of the Catholic Church, Sister Teresa gave back her Sisters of Loreto habit and set out to live in the streets of Calcutta. "That was the biggest sacrifice of my life," she later affirmed. In 1950, she founded an order of nuns called the Missionaries of Charity to provide food for the needy and to operate hospitals, schools, orphanages, youth centres and shelters for lepers and the dying poor. In 1952 she founded the Nirmal Hriday Home for the Dying in a former temple, still in Calcutta. Meaning "the place of the pure heart", this home has welcomed over 65,000 people in the last 30 years and few have left alive. Sister Teresa founded the first home for abandoned babies in Calcutta in 1955, naming it "Children's Home" or *Shishu Bhavan*, in the Bengali language. In 1957 the Missionaries of Charity extended their work with lepers to include victims of AIDS.

Almost 50 years after this young sister decided to progress beyond teaching history and geography to young women, the Missionaries of Charity have grown from twelve sisters in India to over 3,000, in 517 missions throughout 100 countries worldwide.

Mother Teresa, "Saint of the Gutters", was awarded the Nobel Peace Prize in 1979.

103. Reconciling Christians

During his Protestant seminary years in Lausanne, Switzerland, Roger-Louis Schutz-Marsauche had doubts about his faith and about the diversity of denominations in the Christian world. During World War II, he found himself helping Jewish refugees to escape the Nazis, and sheltering them.

Then, in 1949, he returned to the tiny French hamlet of Taizé, south-east of Paris, near Cluny. There "Brother Roger" proceeded to put into operation his spiritual vision of the future: praying and living out the spirit of the gospel with others, and reconciling Christians of all denominations as well as the entire human family. He began with just a handful of brothers representing the Reformed, Lutheran, Anglican and Catholic churches.

But in time the Taizé ecumenical community would grow to 80 brothers. It has since become so internationally known that up to 5,000 people per week make a pilgrimage to the tiny village. These have included Christians, Jews, Buddhists, and even those of no faith.

104. World Vision

In 1949, a young Christian minister and war correspondent named Bob Pierce took five US Dollars from his pocket and handed them to the headmistress of a Chinese missionary school. It was part-payment to allow a ragged, hungry little girl called White Jade to stay at the school, where she would be fed and cared for.

Soon after this, Bob Pierce went to war-torn Korea, where he learned how thousands of suffering people and children orphaned by war were in need of emergency relief in the form of food, water and housing.

Pierce returned to the USA, and in September 1950 he founded World Vision in Portland, Oregon, with the aim of helping orphans, widows and tuberculosis and Hansen's Disease (leprosy) patients, starting in Korea.

Fifty years later, World Vision is the planet's largest privately-funded relief and development organisation, serving well over 50 million people in 103 countries.

105. From filmstar to chaplain

As a young boy in North Dakota, Dick Halverson wanted to become an entertainer when he grew up. He would stand outside the pool hall of the small town of Buchanan and sing for nickels. Later, he toured with a vaudeville troupe. Eventually he made his way to Hollywood, where in 1935 he landed a screen test at Paramount Studios.

But Halverson never turned up for the test. On New Year's Eve 1940, fed up with being alone in his tiny Los Angeles apartment, the young entertainer decided to go to the little church he passed on the way to work every day, Vermont Avenue Presbyterian. Following a prayerful discussion with the pastor, Dick decided to give his life to Jesus Christ.

After theological training, he became minister at the Hollywood Presbyterian Church. After a missionary trip to China in 1948, Halversen met Bob Pierce and decided to join him in developing his World Vision ministry. He continued to work with that organisation for 27 years.

At the same time he wrote 21 books on the Christian life and also wrote and edited a bi-weekly devotional newsletter, called *Perspective*.

Between 1981 and 1995 the man who had once wanted to become a Hollywood film star – now pastor of Fourth Presbyterian Church in Washington, DC – was Chaplain to the US Senate.

106. A candy businessman

Following his graduation in Economics and Sociology from Oklahoma State University, Bill Bright decided to go into business. "At this time, success for me was measured by the accumulation of material possessions, honors, applause and the praise of men," he said. The business in question was the setting up of candy or sweet shops in glamorous "tinseltown": Hollywood. Young Bright's striking resemblance to actor Clark Gable helped him to break into the Hollywood scene. He became a successful businessman.

But his mother's prayers and the persistence of an elderly couple led Bill to attend First Presbyterian Church in Hollywood. In 1945, Bill discovered the gospel of Jesus Christ. Following five years of intensive Bible study at Fuller Theological Seminary at University College of Los Angeles, Bill began to share Christ with students on the campus. In 1951, he set up an organisation called Campus Crusade for Christ (CCC).

The University of California, Berkeley, was the fountainhead of the student revolution during the 1960s. For an entire week, 600 of Bright's CCC staff and students shared the gospel with around 23,000 students. Thousands expressed their desire to receive and follow Jesus.

Half a century later, CCC, still chaired by the ageing Dr Bright and his wife, Vonette, had more than 25,000 full-time staff and over 553,000 trained volunteer staff in 196 countries.

Bright authored over 100 books and booklets as well as thousands of articles and pamphlets. One of CCC's best-known projects was The Jesus Film, about the life of Christ and an hour and a half long. Since its release in 1979, this film has been translated into more than 600 languages. CCC says that more than 4.3 billion people have seen it.

Nor would Bill Bright forget Hollywood. Not long before his death, at his urging, Christian leaders representing 300,000 US churches joined forces to "light a candle" in Hollywood rather than "curse the darkness".

107. Belief recovered

From 1914 until 1930, Cyril EM Joad had been a civil servant whose countless personalised books on philosophy made atheism fashionable. According to Joad, Jesus was only a man, God was part of the universe, and, should the universe be destroyed, God would be destroyed. Joad believed that there was no such thing as sin, and that, given a little time, man would have heaven on earth. His viewpoint was given weight when he was appointed head of the Philosophy Department at Birkbeck College, London.

But, following World War II and with the possibility of a third world conflict in sight, Dr Joad realised that man was sinful. In a complete turnabout, he realised that the only explanation for sin was to be found in the Word of God. The only solution was in the cross of Jesus Christ.

The year before his death in 1952, Cyril Joad published his 48th and final book, which he called *Recovery of Belief*.

108. "That mad priest"

Danilo Dolci's father was a sceptical Sicilian-born station-master, while his mother was a devout Slav. During World War II, Danilo had trained as an architect and engineer in Switzerland. As a student, he published work on the theory of reinforced concrete and was hailed as a man with a brilliant future.

With hostilities over, although not a churchgoer, Danilo was called to work with a priest called Don Zeno at Nomadelphia, a Christian commune in Tuscany caring for war orphans. This included cleaning latrines and hoeing gardens. Don Zeno was so impressed by Danilo that he had him set up another commune, called Ceffarello. But before long the ruling Christian Democrat Party decided that Zeno was a Communist and even the Pope referred to him as "that mad priest". Nomadelphia and Ceffarello were closed down and the orphans placed in government care.

Danilo had once been on holiday in Sicily to study the ancient Greek Doric ruins of Segesta. But then he discovered the wretched state of the island, including the slums of Trappeto, where thousands were surviving in hovels in abject fear of the ruling Mafia. While Danilo was there, a baby died of starvation. In 1952, aged 28, he decided to head for "the poorest place I had ever known". He was to remain there for four decades, winning jobs and water rights away from the Mafia and into the control of local farmers' and craftsmen's collectives.

Having suffered in his youth under Fascist and Nazi rule, Danilo realised that his aims could only be achieved peacefully. So he went on hunger strikes to make the Italian government take notice. In November 1955 he fasted for a week in Partinico "to draw attention to the misery and violence in the area and to promote the building of a dam over the Jato River that could provide irrigation for the entire valley".

On 30th December 1997, Danilo Dolci, "The Sicilian Gandhi", twice a nominee for the Nobel Peace Prize, and once (despite being a non-Communist), the recipient of the Lenin Peace Prize, died at 73 of heart failure – a political maverick to the end.

109. The Samaritans

In 1953, the Reverend Chad Varah was almost too busy to handle any additional work. Vicar of a London suburban church, as well as being a hospital chaplain, he was also a writer and designer for popular teenage comic magazines. When he was not running the youth club or ministering to the aged and sick, Chad was earning extra cash as a journalist.

Then one day Chad read that there were three suicides per day in Greater London. He thought back to his very first action as a priest in 1934: burying a fourteen-year-old girl who'd killed herself when her periods started, thinking she had venereal disease.

Chad decided to do something. He realised that there was no specific telephone number for people to ring if they were considering suicide. A job came up as Vicar of the Church of St Stephen Walbrook, in the heart of the City of London. Chad applied, on condition that he could have an emergency telephone number. He was given both the job and the phone number: MAN 9000. He then persuaded his friends in the world of journalism to publicise his mission.

Chad and his secretary, Vivian, started taking phone calls in

November 1953. With an increasing number of volunteers offering to help man the phone lines and befriend those in need, Varah set up "The Samaritans" the following year.

Ten years after those first calls, in 1963, there were 41 branches of The Samaritans in the UK and Ireland. In 1974, Chad founded Befrienders International and the service went worldwide. By 1993 as many as 23,500 volunteers were answering desperate phone calls around the world, in over 200 branches.

110. Abbé Pierre

Born into a wealthy family of silk-manufacturers, during the Second World War, Henri Groués, code-named "Abbé Pierre", had worked for the French Resistance movement, helping Jewish people to escape into Switzerland. Denounced by the Gestapo, Abbé Pierre fled to North Africa to become part of the Free French. After the war, he returned to France and was elected to the French Parliament for the Meurthe-et-Moselle region. And he might simply have lived out his life as a devoted politician.

But life in post-war France was harsh and there were many homeless and unemployed people. Moved by their situation, Abbé Pierre decided to welcome these people into his own home in the Paris suburb of Neuilly Plaisance. Eighteen homeless men were taken in. The Abbé spent his entire salary buying war surplus materials to enable the erection of temporary homes, initially in his own large garden.

In 1948 he saved from suicide a convict named "Georges" who asked the Abbé to help others like himself. By 1949 "The Ragpickers of Emmaüs" was finally established, financed by the resale of donated items.

In 1954 Abbé Pierre launched an impassioned appeal on French radio, telling how on a cold winter's day a woman was found frozen to death on the streets. This led to an outpouring of charitable donations and prompted government action to help the homeless. Thanks to Abbé Pierre, les Cités d'Urgence and the first HLM council flats were built. Today the Emmaüs movement has a staff of over 4,000 in 30 countries on five continents.

111. A nonsensical gesture of love

During the 1950s, London-born actor Alec Guinness had become a popular star of British-made films such as *Kind Hearts and Coronets*, in which he played the victims of a serial killer, and *The Lavender Hill Mob*, where he played a gold bullion thief. Then, in 1953, Guinness obtained a star part playing the cheerful detective-priest in the film *Father Brown* (*The Detective* in the USA). At this time, Guinness' eleven-year-old son Matthew was paralysed by polio from the waist down. One evening, the actor was walking back in the dark, still in a cassock, to the station hotel of a village near Macon. Suddenly his hand was seized by a small boy, a complete stranger, who called him "mon père" and trotted along beside him, chatting in French.

From then on, as Guinness walked home each night from the film set, he began visiting a Catholic sanctuary, to sit – alone. Finally he made what he called a "negative bargain" with God. If his son Matthew recovered, Guinness vowed never to prevent him from converting. Soon the boy walked, and then ran. The next year, Guinness went on the first of many retreats to Mount St Bernard Abbey.

In his autobiography, *Blessings in Disguise*, the actor

described what followed: "I was walking up Kingsway in the middle of the afternoon when an impulse compelled me to start running. With joy in my heart, and in a state of almost sexual excitement, I ran until I reached the little Catholic church there . . . which I had never entered before. I knelt, caught my breath, and for ten minutes was lost to the world." Guinness was at a loss to explain his actions. He finally decided it was a "rather nonsensical gesture of love", an outburst of thanksgiving for the faith of the ages. On 24th March 1956 Alec Guinness ended his pilgrimage from atheism to Christianity. By 1957, father, mother and son were Christians.

112. "I have a dream . . ."

Martin Luther King Junior's grandfather and father were respectable Baptist pastors in Atlanta, Georgia. King himself had graduated with a divinity degree in 1951, following this with a PhD from Boston University in 1955. At 26 years old, Dr King was serving as pastor of a small Baptist church in Montgomery, Alabama, and had a wife and young child. He was the last man who you might imagine would create any disturbance.

But it was this same Martin Luther King who mobilised the local black community during a 382-day boycott of the city's bus lines. Blacks should have the right to travel on the same buses as whites. Despite arrest, harassment and the bombing of his home, King remained non-violent. He was a great admirer of Gandhi.

Winning the boycott, King gained a national reputation. In 1957 he summoned together a number of black leaders and founded the Southern Christian Leadership Conference. As its president, he travelled 780,000 miles and made 208 speeches in that year alone.

In 1959 Dr King visited India to meet Gandhi's followers, and on returning home he settled down to become a co-pastor with his father of the Ebenezer Baptist Church. But the anti-segregationist movement continued to grow and threatened to become very violent.

In August 1963 some 250,000 supporters joined a march on Washington. At the Lincoln Memorial, King made a speech, remembered since for its key phrase, "I have a dream . . ." ("I have a dream that one day every valley shall be exalted, every hill and mountain shall be made low, the rough places will be made plain, and the crooked places will be made straight, and the glory of the Lord shall be revealed, and all flesh shall see it together.")

The non-violent marches continued. But, in 1968, this youngest man ever to be awarded the Nobel Peace Prize was assassinated. He was only 39 years old.

113. "In five hours I will see Jesus"

Jacques Fesch, a 24-year-old Frenchman and the son of an atheist, had become embittered by life and rejected religious belief. On 25th February 1954 he attempted to steal from a stockbroker to get money so that he and his young family could travel abroad and make a new life. A policeman challenged him, and Jacques accidentally killed him. He was captured and imprisoned. One year later, Jacques had begun his path back to God and his Son, Jesus Christ.

In April 1957, aged 27, Jacques was condemned to death. But it was another five months before the sentence was carried out. Having put his trust in the Lord, on the night before his execution Jacques remarried his wife, Pierrette, in front of a priest. At 4 o'clock the following morning, as he went to his death by guillotine, the young man astonished his executioners with his radiant serenity.

In his last days, Jacques wrote a private journal for his little daughter, Véronique, "for when she will become a woman". This is a complete witness to his trust in Christ. It has since been published, under the title *In five hours I will see Jesus*.

Today Véronique is a nun at the Carmelite Convent of San Remo, Italy.

114. The President's niece

Geneviève de Gaulle was 22 and working in a Paris bookshop when the Gestapo of the occupying Nazi forces arrested her for being in possession of secret documents to do with the Resistance. In 1944 she was deported to the Ravensbrück Concentration Camp outside Berlin, with the possibility of never coming out alive. She survived.

When her uncle became President of the French Republic, Geneviève de Gaulle could have become a relatively well-off, bourgeois housewife. She was married to Bernard Anthonioz, a senior official in the Ministry of Culture. They had four children and lived in a spacious flat near the Jardin de Luxembourg.

But then, in 1958, she met Father Joseph Wresinski. He took her to a shantytown outside Noisy-le-Grand where 260 homeless families were struggling to survive. Shocked by its similarities with Ravensbrück Camp, yet existing so close to Paris, Geneviève de Gaulle-Anthonioz stopped working at the Ministry of Culture to join Father Wresinski in what became ATD-Fourth World.

For the next 35 years she campaigned tirelessly on behalf of the homeless, taking her crusade not only through the Law Courts, but also up to ministerial and presidential levels.

She became the first woman to receive the Great Cross of the Légion d'Honneur.

115. The Hmar New Testament

The Hmars, living in the remote mountain village of Senvon in northern India, were once a savage, head-hunting tribe. In 1916 a Welsh businessman-turned-missionary by the name of Roberts had courageously made the 100-mile seven-day journey to Senvon, to proclaim the gospel of Jesus. Although he had promised to return and open a school and medical clinic, because Roberts had slept in tribal homes and eaten tribal food, thus "demeaning high British culture", the occupying British Army forbade him to go back. As the Hmar had no written language, the only way that those tribesmen who had accepted Christ could carry on was to learn the neighbouring Lushai language, and, having memorised the gospel of St John, return to Senvon to share the good news with their fellows.

One of the sons of those converts was called Rochunga Pudaite. His parents sent him to the nearest upper primary school to study – 96 miles away from their home. Their aim was not that Rochunga might get a good job and provide them with financial security in their old age, but that "you may translate the Bible for us". After he finished middle school, Rochunga went to Jorhat, about 300 miles from home. There he worked as a sweeper, cleaner and gardener in the mission compound to pay for his room and board. After he had finished high school he decided to go to Calcutta to study at St

Paul's College. Once there, the principal told Rochunga that the Indian government had recently set up scholarship funds for tribal students. But then he received bad news from the Ministry of Education: his tribe, the Hmar, was not included in the schedule of tribes of north east India. Denied the scholarship, he wrote a long letter to Pandit Jawaharlal Nehru, Prime Minister of India. Soon afterwards, he received a message from the Prime Minister's office that a scholarship had been arranged for him

When Rochunga finished his arts degree course in Calcutta, he decided to transfer to Allahabad University in the heartland of India. Four months after his graduation from Allahabad, Rochunga was in Glasgow, Scotland, studying Greek and Hebrew. He began translating the Bible. Soon he was offered a scholarship to go to the United States for further training in biblical theology.

In 1958, 16 years after leaving the mountainous jungle, Rochunga returned home with his newly-translated Hmar New Testament. It was published in 1960 and became the Hmar bestseller: the first 5,000 sold out in six months.

Rochunga's prayers and those of his parents had been answered.

116. Brother Andrew

In 1949, 21-year-old Andrew van der Bejl enlisted as a volunteer soldier, a commando, to go out and fight in Indonesia, then a Dutch colony. He was hit by a bullet and seriously injured, and faced a lengthy convalescence. It was then that Andrew discovered that the greatest battle he faced was the one raging within his soul. The kind smile and personal testimony of Christ's love from one of the hospital sisters led him to accept Jesus as his Lord and Saviour. "A bullet made an end to my sports ambition, but put me on the track to Jesus."

Conversion "did not come suddenly". It grew from reading the Bible, and seeking God. He went to Glasgow in 1953 to study at a Worldwide Evangelization Mission College. But it was while attending a Communist youth festival in Warsaw, Poland that he felt a decisive call to the mission field. Adopting the name Brother Andrew, he began loading up his blue Volkswagen Beetle with Bibles, and courageously started smuggling them into nearly every country in the Communist Bloc: Poland, East Germany, Czechoslovakia, Yugoslavia, Hungary, Bulgaria . . . then finally into Russia itself, the centre of the Soviet Union and the very stronghold of atheism.

Brother Andrew's book, *God's Smuggler*, sold 10 million copies in over 30 countries and helped to internationalise his ministry, Open Doors, at the Service of Persecuted Christians. This led to offices in 20 countries, 200 full-time workers, and thousands of volunteers. Millions of Bibles have been taken into over 60 countries where Christianity is still either prohibited or severely sanctioned. In 1981, for "Project Pearl", one million Bibles were smuggled into China in a single night on a custom-built barge carrying 232 tons of the Word of God! More recently, Brother Andrew has turned his attention to Christians in the Arab World. In some Muslim countries it is illegal to own a Bible, pray aloud, or wear a cross, and punishment can range from flogging to imprisonment to execution.

In 1997, this former Dutch commando was honoured by the World Evangelical Fellowship as "legendary".

117. A spear-killer hears the gospel

The Missionary Aviation Fellowship was not without its dangers, and even tragedy. In January 1956, five young North Americans – Nate Saint, Jim Elliot, Roger Youderian, Pete Fleming and Ed McCully – took off in a Piper aircraft. Their mission: to make peaceful contact with the stone-age tribe known to the outside world as the feared and hated Aucas. Living in the rugged Amazon rainforests on the eastern flanks of the Andes mountains of Ecuador, this tribe was known for its violent contacts with the outside world, as well as for the habitual spear-killings within the tribe. Things went wrong and the MAF team were killed by several Aucas, led by one called Gikita. The little yellow plane was left, stripped and ruined, as a monument to the awesome task of sharing a message of peace and forgiveness with peoples who have no concept of a loving and benevolent God.

Two years later, Nate Saint's sister, Rachel, and Jim Elliot's widow, Elisabeth, with her little girl Valerie, were invited by Gikita's sister into the Auca territory to live among their relatives' killers. Eventually, Gikita heard of Wangongi, the Man Maker, and Itota, his only Son, from the two "cowodi" women whose men he himself had speared to death. In time, he and many of his fellow tribesmen became Christians.

118. The Cross and the Switchblade

In 1959, David Wilkerson, a 28-year-old Pennsylvanian country pastor, happened to see a photo in *Life* magazine of several New York teenagers who had been charged with murder. At this time, violent gangs ruled by warlords, drug pushers and pimps held the streets of New York's ghettos – Manhattan, the Bronx and Brooklyn – in an iron grip. Pastor Wilkerson travelled to New York and arrived with nothing more than a Bible.

From experience, he gradually found the way to show members of these gangs that Jesus loved them. Eventually even the most hardened leader, Nicky Cruz, gave his life to Christ. Wilkerson co-authored a book *The Cross and the Switchblade* about his New York mission. It has been read by over 50 million people in some 30 languages and 150 countries. A motion picture was also released.

Wilkerson went on to found Teen Challenge Ministries, which was to grow to 490 outreach centres, with an 86% success rate in helping addicts turn away from drugs. Even in his seventies, the pastor would go out alone or sometimes with an assistant to walk through the streets of New York City, along Broadway and Eighth Avenue or down 42nd Street and nearby "Crack Alley" on 41st Street. His mission was always to seek out the lost, the disorientated and the addicted, to tell them of the power of the risen Christ to set them free.

119. "God of the universe, I believe again!"

As a boy, Alexander Solzhenitsyn planned to find fame through commemorating the bloody glories of the Bolshevik Revolution. But, as an artillery captain in World War II, he privately criticised Stalin and got packed off for eight years to the "gulags", the concentration camps where any further thoughts of resistance ought to have been brainwashed out of him. But Solzhenitsyn resisted. This previously loyal Leninist met luminous religious believers and moved from the Marx of his schoolteachers to the Jesus of his Russian Orthodox forefathers: "God of the Universe!" he wrote. "I believe again! Though I renounced You, You were with me!"

On his release, Solzhenitsyn began to write books about the horrors of Soviet prison life. This included scolding Soviet leaders for their attempted eradication of Christian religion and morality. For this, the Kremlin sent him to the West in 1974. But, once in the USA, he admonished Western élites for discarding "the moral heritage of Christian centuries with their great reserves of mercy and sacrifice", and for substituting "the proclaimed and practised autonomy of man from any higher force above him".

120. Jesus rediscovered

From the 1930s, Malcolm Muggeridge had built up a very lively but controversial reputation as an author, newspaper journalist and television broadcaster. He was known as a socialist and an agnostic. Muggeridge was a self-professed "religious maniac without a religion", declaring, "I don't believe in the resurrection of Christ, I don't believe that he was the Son of God in a Christian sense", and adding that he was "enchanted by a religion I cannot believe".

But in the 1960s Muggeridge went to Calcutta to produce a BBC TV documentary about Mother Teresa and the "Missionaries of Charity".

This documentary, entitled *Something Beautiful for God*, was one of a sequence of elements which gradually led to Muggeridge's conversion to Christianity. He described this in his book *Jesus Rediscovered*:

> My evangelical friends are always rather disappointed that I can't produce a sort of a Damascus road experience – you know, that I

was such a person and then suddenly this happened and I was such another person. But I can't.

In November 1982, the 79-year-old journalist and his wife, Kitty, to whom he had been married for 54 years, became members of the Roman Catholic Church. From then on, all "Saint Mugg's" writings concerned the Christian experience.

121. A fast-food entrepreneur

James B Cathy, a real estate agent, had been ruined twice, first by the Great Depression in 1929 and then by a boll-weevil plague that destroyed the cotton crop in rural Georgia, USA. While never encouraged to go to church, nor even shown any paternal love, his son Truett did find love – and a belief in Jesus Christ – from his mother, Lilla Kimbell.

Following military service during World War II, S Truett Cathy decided to go into the restaurant business. He opened his first *Chick-fil-A* restaurant in 1967. Thirty-five years later, *Chick-fil-A* had become the third largest quick-service chicken restaurant company in the USA, with over 725 outlets, mainly in shopping malls, in 35 states, as well as in South Africa and Canada.

At around the same time as he was starting up his fast-food business, Cathy began teaching teenagers at Sunday school. This also grew, to the extent that, in 1984, he founded the WinShape Center Foundation to work towards "shaping winners" by helping young people succeed in life through scholarships and other youth support programmes. This came to include nine foster care homes in Georgia, Alabama, Tennessee and Brazil, with plans to add at least one new foster home each year. In 1995, more than 1,500 young people from twelve states attended Camp WinShape summer camps. Two years later, S Truett Cathy was appointed Chairman of the National Bible Week in recognition of all the work he had done.

122. Rock star with a Christian banner

In 1959, Cliff Richard and his rock-and-roll pop group, "The Shadows", recorded a song entitled "Living Doll". It rocketed to the top of the Hit Parade and the group was soon proclaimed as Britain's answer to American rock. For the next seven years, Cliff Richard and The Shadows had hundreds of thousands of teenagers swooning and screaming to their music.

By 1966, Cliff had notched up his eighth number-one single and become a millionaire. But then, on 16th June of that year, the American evangelist Billy Graham held a rally before a packed audience at Earl's Court, London. As usual, Dr Graham invited people in the audience to come forward and declare their faith. When the news was published that Cliff Richard was among them, many of his rock fans wept.

But from then on, Cliff Richard's attitude in his recorded songs, albums and pop concerts would be, "If I'm going to represent God, I have to do it to the best I can. So I still go as far as I can into rock and roll carrying my Christian banner."

In 2004, Sir Cliff was still raising that banner high.

123. Tortured for Christ

During the 1930s, Richard Wurmbrand, who had been born into a Jewish family in Bucharest, Romania, was a stockbroker with atheist opinions. But then, following a long bout of tuberculosis, while on holiday with his Jewish wife, Sabrina, Wurmbrand met a German carpenter called Wolfkes, who interested the couple in the life of Jesus Christ. The New Testament accounts so impressed this Jewish couple that, with encouragement from a Jewish friend who had become a Christian, they became Christians and formed a mission to the Jews in Bucharest.

Following imprisonment and release by the Nazis, Richard Wurmbrand was kidnapped by the Communist Police in 1948. They gave him a different name and attempted to wipe out his Christian beliefs by torture and brainwashing, including three whole years in solitary confinement. His wife met with similar treatment.

Following a payment to the Communists by Christian-Jewish organisations and the "underground church", Wurmbrand was released. He had 18 deep scars on his neck, chest and back.

Then Richard Wurmbrand wrote a book, *Tortured for Christ*, which was subsequently published and translated into many languages. In 1967 he founded the "Voice of the Martyrs" to highlight Christian persecution in China and in nations controlled by Islamic fundamentalists. In 1990 the Wurmbrands returned to Bucharest after 25 years, to preach about love and forgiveness.

124. Joni

As a teenager, Joni Eareckson loved life. She enjoyed riding horses and loved to swim. In the summer of 1967, however, all that changed. While swimming with some friends on a hot afternoon in Chesapeake Bay, Joni dived into a lake, not knowing how shallow it really was. She broke her neck, paralysing her body from the neck down. Lying in her hospital bed, she tried desperately to make sense of the horrible turn of events.

> I begged friends to assist me in suicide. Slit my wrists, dump pills down my throat, anything to end my misery! And questions! I had so many. I believed in God, but I was angry with Him.

Then a friend told Joni about Jesus Christ's suffering on the cross. For the next two years, during her rehabilitation, Joni struggled. She struggled with life, she struggled with God, and she struggled with her paralysis. She spent long months learning how to paint with a brush between her teeth. After that she never looked back. Today she writes, paints, sings, drives a car, and gives glory to God – all without the use of her hands or legs!

In 1975, Joni's autobiography, simply called *Joni*, became a bestseller, and a feature film based on it has been translated into fifteen languages and shown in scores of countries around the world, many of which Joni has visited personally. On the strength of this, she founded "Joni and Friends" to help disabled people worldwide.

In 1982, Joni married a teacher called Ken Tada, who would soon give up his job to help Joni and Friends.

Apart from writing over 30 books (such as *All God's Children*), Joni became a columnist for major Christian magazines around the world. She was named "Churchwoman of the Year" in 1993 by the Religious Heritage Foundation and was the first woman to be honoured by the National Association of Evangelicals as their "Layperson of the Year".

In 2002, Joni and Friends served over 500 special-needs families through nine family retreats across the USA. Through Wheels for the World, over 14,000 wheelchairs have been collected across the USA, refurbished by inmates in correctional facilities, and shipped to developing nations where physical therapists fit each chair to a needy disabled child or adult. *Joni and Friends*, a daily five-minute radio programme, is heard in over 850 broadcast outlets across America and this year received the "Radio Program of the Year" award from National Religious Broadcasters. Through ten area offices, Joni and Friends teams provide church training and education to promote the inclusion of people with disabilities.

125. Chasing the Dragon

In the 1960s, Jackie Pullinger was a competent music student from a comfortable, middle-class background in the suburbs of London. Then she decided to give her life to Christ and become a missionary. Yet all her applications to missionary societies were rejected. There was no need for a musician. So an East London vicar advised her to take the cheapest ship on the longest route passing through the most countries, and during that voyage to pray to the Lord to direct her. Her prayers were answered.

In 1966, Jackie arrived in the British Protectorate of Hong Kong. Before long she was working inside the notorious Walled City of Kowloon, with its drug-addiction-based child prostitution and gambling dens terrorised by Triad gangs.

But "Poon Siu Jeh", as they called her, began to pray "in tongues" for and with these people to stop their habit and give their lives to Jesus. During the following decade, hundreds of young Hong-Kong people kicked their drug addiction and became Christians: even the hardened leaders of the Walled City Triads.

Jackie Pullinger's book *Chasing the Dragon* became a best-seller.

126. Refugee businessman

In 1967, 16-year-old Balram Gidoomal and his family escaped to Britain as refugees from Kenya, along with their Hindu idols and very little money. Balram had to call on all his business experience and entrepreneurial flair to rebuild his shattered life and business interests. Within six months he had already become the owner of six shops.

It was while studying at London University that Ram became a Christian.

During the next 20 years Ram built up his business "Winning Communication", a consultancy specialising in leadership training and equal opportunities. By the late 1980s it was worth $130 million and employed some 7,000 people. It was at this time that Ram launched a charity, "Christmas Cracker", to help and support poor people in the slums of India.

In 1992 he stepped down from his business, but continued his services to the Asian community and race relations, including the New Deal Task Force Ethnic Minority Advisory Group, as well as South Asian Concern. This is part of the EMA (Evangelical Missionary Alliance) and backs Christian missionaries both in England and in India to convert Hindus. Ram is also a member of the Christian People's Alliance, which is a wing of the Christian Democratic party and dominant in many European countries.

127. Shantytown missionary

Marie-Madeleine Cinquin was born in Brussels in 1908. Terribly disturbed by the death of her father, she was ordained a nun with the Congregation of Notre-Dame de Sion in Jerusalem in 1928, becoming a teacher of philosophy and taking the name of Sœur Emmanuelle. She then left for Istanbul, where she would remain for 28 years. She moved to war-torn Algeria for five years, and finally to Alexandria, in Egypt.

In 1970, aged 62, she should have retired. Instead, she decided to devote herself to looking after children in d'Azbet-et-Nakhl, a poor shantytown of Cairo, amongst the rubbish-collectors and the rag-pickers living on the fringes of society, literally upon the piles of refuse and garbage that were collected from the city every day.

In 1979 Sœur Emmanuelle decided to tour the world to raise the first million dollars for her Egyptian protégés, with the help of associations that sprang up in France, Belgium and Switzerland at her request

By the age of 74, Sœur Emmanuelle, still living and working in a squalid suburb called Mokattam, had delegated and extended her activities to other countries such as the Sudan, Libya, the Philippines and Haiti. Since then, "Les Amis de Sœur Emmanuelle" have come to help as many as 60,000 children throughout the world.

In 1993, Sœur Emmanuelle's superiors ordered her to return to France. But, even in her eighties, this indefatigable lady became concerned about the homeless in southern France, while also writing three books, including *Le Paradis C'est les Autres*.

128. Insignificant astronauts

Although his mother had wanted James B Irwin to be a preacher, a brief ride in an old barnstorming biplane in 1934 turned the four-year-old boy's mind to flying. Following training in the no-nonsense businesses of naval science and aeronautical engineering during the early 1960s, Irwin had become a highly experienced test pilot for the US Air Force. He accumulated over 7,000 hours flying time, 5,300 of them in jet aircraft. In 1966, NASA selected Irwin as one of the 19 astronauts who would crew the *Apollo* missions to the moon. In July 1971, Irwin was one of three men who took *Apollo 15* to land on the moon and drive the Lunar Rover 1 across its surface, collecting 175 lbs of rock and soil. It is estimated that they brought back as much scientific information as Charles Darwin acquired during his five-year voyage in *The Beagle* in 1831–1836.

But, as astronaut Irwin looked into the inky blackness and saw the Earth suspended in space, he was deeply moved: "I felt the power of God as I've never felt it before."

In July 1972 Irwin resigned from NASA to form a religious organisation, the High Flight Foundation, based in Colorado Springs, to organise religious retreats and tours of the Holy Land.

Irwin was not alone. *Apollo 16*'s team in 1972 included another hardened pilot, astronaut Charlie Duke. Duke also drove the Lunar Module around the moon's surface for a considerable number of hours. Retiring from NASA in 1975, Duke remained in the US Air Force Reserve but also went into business, including directorships and his own company, Charlie Duke Enterprises. But at the same time he became an active Christian lay worker, speaking at numerous churches. He is president of Duke Ministry for Christ.

"I felt insignificant faced with the immensity of the Divine Creation," he later recalled.

129. Two Vietnam war victims

In 1972, while serving in the Vietnam War, John Plummer set up an air strike on the village of Trang Bang, having twice been assured that there were no civilians in the area. Soon afterwards, he saw a photo of nine-year-old Kim Phuc running, naked and horribly burned by napalm, from that very village. This photo became famous as an anti-war image.

Returning home a broken man, Plummer ignored God, took to drink, got divorced from his wife and left his four children. Several years later he met and married Joanne, who led him to Christ in 1990. He became a Methodist minister.

Unknown to Plummer, Kim Phuc had survived her burns, become a pharmacologist, married and defected to Canada. She too had become a Christian.

Then, in 1996, the least likely thing happened. John Plummer and Kim Phuc were reunited at a Vietnam Veterans' Day in Washington. He was able to ask her forgiveness and she to forgive him.

130. Outreach café in Dresden

Now in her seventies, Sabine Ball runs a Christian café for young people in the Szene suburb of Dresden. The clientele ranges from junkies to punks to neo-Nazis, and they come for inexpensive coffee, second-hand goods and a chance to chat about the message of Jesus.

Although Sabine was born in Dresden, after World War II she emigrated to America. After obtaining a job at a yacht club on Florida's Miami Beach, Sabine met and married multi-millionaire Clifford Ball in 1952. When they were not hosting endless cocktail parties at their luxury villa in Florida, the Balls were going on extended luxury cruises. But when Clifford became an alcoholic, Sabine left him and their children in search of something else. She sold her wardrobe and gold jewellery, and bought a remote farm, where she smoked hash and took strong drugs with a group of hippies. In her search for meaning, she spent a summer at a Buddhist monastery in Kathmandu, meditating for five hours a day but convinced that there was no God.

Returning to the USA in 1972, aged 42, she met a 26-year-old Christian who spent many hours explaining the gospel to her and sharing Christ's message of love. Soon afterwards, Sabine went to live and work in the slums of Brooklyn, New York, sharing the word of Christ with drug addicts and prostitutes.

In 1992, while making a return visit to her native Dresden, Sabine came across many godless young people whose lives were dominated by pornography, psychic phenomena and violence. It was then that she decided to stay on and to establish the "Café Metabolism".

131. Professor helps poor peasants

Adolfo Perez Esquival was an established professor of architecture and a sculptor in his native Buenos Aires, Argentina, and also a Christian.

But in 1974, aged 43, he gave up his teaching post and began travelling to Ecuador, Bolivia, Paraguay, Brazil and Honduras to work for peace with local movements, often aiding poor peasants in their struggles against rich landowners. Esquival was arrested twice, the second time in Argentina in 1977, where he was detained for 14 months without a trial and was subjected to psychological and physical torture. On release, he founded *El Servizio Paz y Justicia*, a human-rights organisation. Adolfo Esquival's passion for peace and his love of the people of Latin America earned him the 1980 Nobel Peace Prize. In his acceptance speech he said:

> Because of our faith in Christ and humankind, we must apply our humble efforts to the construction of a more just and humane world. And I want to declare emphatically: Such a world is possible. . . . We know that peace is only possible when it is a fruit of justice. True peace is the result of the profound transformation effected by non-violence, which is, indeed, the power of love.

132. Biker to bikers

In 1972, Herb Shreve, a Baptist pastor from Hatfield, Arkansas, was driving along a country road, concerned about how he could establish a bridgehead with his rebellious 16-year-old son, Herbie. When several motorcycles roared past him, he got an idea. He went out and bought two motorcycles, one for his son and the other for himself. Together they hit the road.

Two years later they went to a motorcycle rally and encountered a group of bikers who did not know about the gospel of Jesus. Pastor Herb prayed, "Please God, send someone to help these people. But please . . . don't let it be me." But, in the end, he realised that he was the one. In 1975, the Shreves set up the non-profit-making, Christian Motorcyclists Association (CMA).

Many hardcore bikers may have looked askance at the CMA riders and their brand of fellowship. But soon letters were pouring in, asking for more information, and CMA began to expand. Today there are 88,000 members in the USA in more than 600 state chapters, including about 150 members in five Utah chapters from Logan to Price. Staff evangelists, who each oversee a multi-state region, average 40,000 to 60,000 miles a year on their machines.

CMA (UK) and CMA South Africa soon followed – and CMA International is now thriving. Among the events is the "Run For The Son", where bikers assemble to raise money for charity.

Jesus said, "Go into the highways and hedges, compelling all to come in that my house might be full" (Luke 14:23).

133. Atheist becomes pastor

Monsieur and Madame Busson, workers in a Paris suburb, had brought up their son Alain as an atheist. He grew up to be a militant member of the Communist Party and the CGT (Confédération Générale du Travail), studying at a Marxist university. Then, aged 21, Alain Busson was looking after sheep while working at an Israeli kibbutz in Galilee when he met a Christian Englishwoman who talked to him about Jesus. Until then Alain had thought that Christians made people believe in another world so as to take better advantage of those down here. But the biblical prophecies fascinated him. One day he was feeding the lambs on the kibbutz when he suddenly had the overpowering feeling of being deeply loved. He distinctly heard the message, "He is alive!"

Raifä, a missionary pastor in Israel planned Alain's return to France. An American mission financed three of the five years he spent studying theology. He then became a pastor, deep in the French rural region of Ariège. He later returned to Israel to reflect and pray in the desert alongside the Red Sea. Back in France, before being accepted by the Taizé community, Brother Roger told Alain to return to civilian life for six months. While working in advertising, Alain deepened his knowledge of the Lutheran Church and became a Protestant.

During the thirteen years that followed, he served as a Lutheran pastor in the Montbéliard region, where he became a prison visitor. Then, in 2002, aged 53, Alain Busson was ordained in Elsau Prison, in front of 80 inmates and 30 people from outside the prison. Two inmates took part in the prayers and Bible readings.

134. Gospel for native tribes

The Reverend Tom Claus is a Mohawk Indian from the Sixth National Iroquois Confederacy in Ontario, Canada. From the 1950s onwards Tom was working among Native American people forced to live either in city slums or on reservations, deprived of native pride and often taking to crime because of alcoholism and drug abuse.

Then, in March 1975, Tom felt "led of the Lord" to call together more than 100 Christian Native leaders from North America's ancient tribes to participate in the Conference on Christian Indian Fellowship in Evangelism, held in Albuquerque, New Mexico.

Out of the prayers of this conference was born CHIEF – Christian Hope Indian Eskimo Fellowship. Its mission was to raise up trained Native American Christian leaders and bring the words of Christ to the 51.1 million Indians of the 1,200 native tribes, with their 250 different languages, throughout the western hemisphere. In 1987, in order to accomplish this goal, CHIEF established the Chief Shepherd Discipleship Center on an eight-acre campus in north Phoenix, Arizona.

As part of his mission, Tom Claus spoke at many public

open-air meetings. At one such, in Syracuse, NY, wearing a full-feathered head-dress, Tom declared that, despite the history of broken treaties and genocide against native peoples, he did not hate the white man, because the white man brought him to Jesus – and he would "rather have Jesus than all the land in the US". This was met with wild cheering. A song with its lyrics flashed on a giant screen describing "one Holy race".

While CHIEF's present ministry covers the Americas, their most recent endeavour has been to take the gospel to Mongolian tribes between China and Russia. From one believer, there are now over 1,000 Mongolian Christians.

135. Born again – the President's hatchet man

During the early 1970s, Charles W Colson was not thinking about reaching out to prison inmates or reforming the US penal system. In fact, this aide to US President Richard Nixon was "incapable of humanitarian thoughts", but capable of dirty tricks and willing to do almost anything for the cause of his president and his party. Colson was known as the White House "hatchet man", a man feared by even the most power-ful politicians during his four years of service to President Nixon.

But not long after Nixon had been forced to resign follow-ing the Watergate scandal, Colson became a Christian. When this news was leaked to the press, *The Boston Globe* com-mented, "If Mr Colson can repent of his sins, there just has to be hope for everybody."

Today, Chuck Colson is considered to be one of America's leading authorities on the causes of and responses to crime. He has addressed nearly half the state legislatures in America and has met with a large number of governors. He is a syndicated columnist and has contributed articles to magazines and newspapers such as *The Wall Street Journal, USA Today, The Washington Post* and *The Chicago Tribune.* Colson provides a daily radio commentary, *BreakPoint,* which airs on 1,000 radio networks to a weekly listening audience of three million people. He is a sought-after speaker. *Born Again,* Colson's first book, was published in 1976 and became an international bestseller. Since then he has written 37 more books. He donates his royalties to Prison Fellowship Ministries, an outreach to convicts, victims of crime, and justice officers.

136. A co-inventor and creationist

In 1977, the world's first scanner using MRI (Magnetic Resonance Imaging) went into action. Using advanced principles of physics and computing, it lets doctors visualise organs such as heart, lungs, chest and their diseased parts without the risks of exploratory surgery or the radiation associated with traditional scanning methods. Today MRI is a world-famous, multi-billion-dollar technology, with more than 5,000 of these complex machines installed around the world.

The inventor of MRI, hailed as one of the greatest diagnostic breakthroughs ever, is Dr Raymond V Damadian. Apart from his international reputation as a scientist, Dr Damadian is not only a highly accomplished violinist, but also a committed Christian who is convinced of the scientific truth of Genesis creation and its fundamental importance to church and society. As a "super scientist", Dr Damadian has spoken out publicly in favour of the Creation science ministry.

137. God's microphone

Oscar Romero was a Roman Catholic clergyman in the highly repressive regime in El Salvador. In 1970 he was made bishop, and then seven years later, aged 60, he was elected archbishop, although considered as a compromise candidate for his fellow bishops. Predictably, as an orthodox pious "bookworm", Bishop Oscar had even been known to criticise those seeking greater freedom.

But then, three weeks after his election, Archbishop Romero's first priest was ambushed and killed alongside two parishioners – an old man and a boy – for having defended peasants' rights to organise farm co-operatives. Romero went down to the village church and publicly showed them solidarity. Some 200 of those who had attended were later killed.

Over 75,000 Salvadorans would be killed, one million would flee the country and another million would be left homeless, constantly on the run from the army – and all this in a country of only 5.5 million. All Romero had to offer the people were weekly homilies broadcast throughout the country, his voice assuring them not that atrocities would cease, but that the church of the poor, ie they themselves, would live on.

> If some day they take away the radio station from us . . . if they don't let us speak, if they kill all the priests and the bishop too, and you are left a people without priests, each one of you must become God's microphone, each one of you must become a prophet.

In 1980, amidst increasing violence, Romero wrote to President Jimmy Carter, pleading with him to cease sending military aid because, he wrote, "it is being used to repress my people". His letter went unheeded.

On 23rd March Romero was shot down during mass. He had openly challenged an army of peasants, whose high command feared and hated his reputation. Ending a long homily broadcast throughout the country, his voice rose to breaking point: "Brothers, you are from the same people; you kill your fellow peasant . . . No soldier is obliged to obey an order that is contrary to the will of God . . . "

138. Boxer spreads the gospel

In 1973, 24-year-old US professional boxer "Big George" Foreman aggressively fought Smokin' Joe Frazier for the Heavyweight Championship of the World. He knocked Frazier to the canvas six times before a second round knockout victory. In March of the following year, Foreman successfully defended his title against Ken Norton but seven months later lost it to Muhammad Ali in the famous "Rumble in the Jungle" in Kinshasa, Zaïre, now Democratic Republic of Congo.

In 1977, after losing only his second fight to Jimmy Young, Foreman had an experience in his dressing room that was to change his life to the extent that he retired and returned to Houston, where he became an evangelical minister in a small church, and established a youth and community centre.

In 1987, needing money to support his family and his centre, George Foreman decided to return to boxing ten years after leaving it. He fought Evander Holyfield for the heavyweight title in 1991, and lost. But he persisted in his comeback. In 1994, two months short of his 46th birthday, he knocked out Thomas Moorer and won back the championship. He became the oldest man ever to hold the heavyweight title. George can still be found spreading the gospel in Houston, Texas.

139. The *Anastasis*

In 1964, the Bahamas were devastated by a hurricane. During a meeting, one of the Youth With a Mission groups prayed for a ship that could bring help after similar disasters. The idea stuck with one of the outreach leaders, Don Stephens. Fourteen years later, a 522-foot former luxury cruise liner, the *Victoria*, was purchased by the organisation that Stephens had co-founded, Mercy Ships. It was renamed the *Anastasis* and was soon refitted with operating theatres, dental facilities and storage space.

By 1998, Mercy Ships had a fleet of four. Over the previous 25 years, voluntary workers on board these vessels, which cruised between the Third World ports, had treated over 300,000 patients in village medical and dental clinics. They had delivered thousands of tons of relief materials, including medical equipment, hospital supplies and medicines. Over 250 construction and agricultural projects had been completed.

140. Growth despite persecution

By the late 1970s, the Chinese Communist Party admitted that the Cultural Revolution had been a disaster. Mao no longer had god-like status. The new leader, Deng Xiao Ping, decided to release thousands of intellectuals from long, hard years in labour camps where every attempt had been made to force their beliefs into conformity with those of the state.

Among those released were several frail old men, who at first sight would have appeared to present no new threat to the state. Their names were Wang Ming Dao, Ling Xiangao

(Samuel Lamb) and Yuan Xiangchen (Allen Yuan). Back in the 1950s, in an effort to distance religion from what it saw as foreign, imperialist influences, the new Communist government had formed The Three-Self Patriotic Movement for Protestant Christians. It was to be "self-supporting, self-governing and self-propagating", all under the watchful eye of the government's Religious Affairs Bureau. The idea was that all organisations, religious or secular, had to be led by the Communist Party.

Eleven Christian preachers, including Wang Ming Dao, Ling Xiangao (Samuel Lamb) and Yuan Xiangchen (Allen Yuan), had refused to join the movement. One said that a church that weds itself to a government, particularly a Communist government, is a whore. So they were separated from their families and sent off to labour camps, where they remained for the next 20 years.

As soon as they were released, in the late 1970s, this small band of aged Christians each began to organise house churches in Beijing. These were not registered with the Religious Affairs Bureau. In time, the congregations of these house churches swelled to 900. On one occasion, 16 policemen came to pastor Samuel Lamb's house church. They closed the church, and took away ten tape recorders, 10,000 tapes, hymnals and Bibles. They removed all his closed circuit TVs, which allowed the people in different parts of the house to see him when he preached. Pastor Lamb was questioned at the police station for 21 hours. But he did not give up. Soon he was preaching to 1,200 people at four different services every week. "Suffering is good for us!" he said. "Persecution good! More persecution, more growing!"

The Chinese government has not been able to stop him. He is so well known that they are careful what they do when it comes to harassing him.

141. Jazz musician walks away from lucrative career

For ten years John Wimber had built a reputation as a popular jazz keyboard player with rock bands in nightclubs. By 1963, he had become manager of the successful "Righteous Brothers" singing duo, Bobby Hatfield and Bill Medley, who had chart-topping hits including "You've Lost That Loving Feeling".

Then, in April 1963, the group's drummer, who with his wife had become a Christian, invited John and Carol Wimber to attend their Bible study group. Within weeks, following "total mental confusion and emotional frustration", John Wimber decided to walk away from his lucrative career and accept Jesus. During the next decade he became an enthusiastic evangelist, leading many to follow Christ.

In 1978, Wimber began pastoring a small fellowship of 150 in Yorba Linda, California, which had been started up by a young pastor called Kenn Gulliksen. Known as Vineyard Christian Fellowship, by 1982, under Wimber's leadership, more than 1,000 people were bursting the seams of the high school gym in which they were meeting.

142. Soviet dissident refuses to compromise

On 27th April 1979, in New York City, the USSR exchanged five Soviet dissidents detained in or sentenced to jail as opponents of the government for two Russian citizens convicted of spying in the United States. Among those dissidents was a most unlikely candidate by the name of Georgi Vins. At the time of his release, thousands of American and Canadian

Christians were wearing "Friends of the West" prayer bracelets that carried his name.

Georgi Vins had been halfway through a second ten-year prison term in a Siberian gulag (forced labour camp) when he was flown to the USA. Indeed, since the mid-1960s Comrade Vins had been arrested several times and made to work in concentration camps in the Ural Mountains, at a factory in the Ukraine, and then in Siberia, where he had been living for fifteen years.

Vins had refused to compromise his stand against the 1929 Soviet Legislation Regarding Religious Cults, which required all religious groups to be registered with the government. This meant restrictions that would destroy the church: no charitable work, no Bible studies and no meetings for children, women and young people.

Vins well knew the price of resistance. His father, the Reverend Peter, had died in a Siberian concentration camp in 1943, following several periods of imprisonment for preaching the word of Christ.

Yet even this and his own imprisonment did not stop Georgi from setting up an Evangelical Baptist Church network of some 2,000 persecuted congregations across the USSR.

Just before his exile to the United States, a Soviet official told Georgi Vins he would never again set foot on Soviet soil. That prediction came true. When he returned to his homeland in 1990, the Soviet Union had ceased to exist and Christian worship was once again tolerated.

143. Book changes addict's life

Angie Taylor was a heroin addict, prostitute, alcoholic, ex-prison convict, mental-hospital patient and street-dweller.

After 16 years of addiction and living rough, Angie, ridden with lice, eating from dustbins and selling her body for a can of lager, wanted to die. Her liver was swelling from self-neglect and abuse. In her usual alcoholic haze, Angie was sitting on a bench outside the Salvation Army hall in Sutton, England, drinking a cup of tea. She has no recollection of how a copy of *The Book of Common Prayer* from a Salvation Army jumble sale came to be in her hands. "I probably stole it," she says candidly. But the book changed her life.

As she idly thumbed through its pages – dimly remembering her church upbringing – a piece of paper fell out onto the ground. It was a picture of Jesus wearing a crown of thorns. That image changed Angie's life. She never took heroin or touched alcohol again. All her addictions completely stopped. She went to the DSS and asked for money to clean herself up. The distinct and obvious change in her life and attitude later convinced the authorities to find her accommodation. More than anything else Angie wanted to be reunited with her children, who were then living with her mother. Angie took a word-processing course and worked as a temp until a permanent position arose. After many traumas and difficulties, she was eventually reconciled with her children. Her son, however, was later killed in a work accident. Angie needed all her new-found Christian faith to cope with the deep hurt and sorrow that ensued.

Life has turned full circle now. She married the widowed pastor of her church fellowship and became stepmother to five young children. This has helped greatly to compensate Angie for the loss of her own children. From their home in Cornwall, the couple are busily engaged in rehabilitation work with drug addicts and marriage counselling. Angie is now a Methodist preacher. She travels the country, telling all kinds of people about her experiences and God's power to change lives. One journey involved walking from John O' Groats to Land's End, carrying an eleven-foot cross to attract attention to the Christian faith.

"It's amazing that God could turn someone who had sunk so low into a means of blessing and helping other people. Only God could do that."

144. Rescuing babies in Bangladesh

During the 1970s, in the aftermath of a liberation war in Bangladesh, many children and babies had been abandoned. An orphanage had been started in Dhaka, but it lacked the necessary resources.

Pat Kerr was one of the many elegantly uniformed air stewardesses working for British Airways, giving passengers newspapers, drinks and tray-meals. Then, in 1981, she visited Bangladesh for the first time. Following a visit to the Dhaka orphanage, she began working as a volunteer while on stopovers. When the orphanage was threatened with closure, Pat Kerr appealed to the chairman, cabin crews and staff of British Airways to raise the money for a new home. The Dhaka Orphanage Project, in conjunction with UNICEF, raised nearly a million pounds, and Sreepur Children's Village was opened in 1989 as a replacement for Dhaka. Since then, Sreepur has given care and hope to almost 1,000 destitute children and their mothers. It has its own school, clinic, market garden, fish farm and training workshops.

Pat Kerr writes all about it in the book *Down to Earth*.

145. In memory of Sam

In 1983, Samantha Smith, a ten-year-old girl from the small town of Manchester, Maine, USA, wrote a short letter to

Soviet leader Yuri Andropov. In it she asked for world peace and finished with "God made the world for us to live together in peace and not to fight."

Portions of this letter were published in the Communist official newspaper, *Pravda*. This was the tense time of the Cold War between the USSR and the USA. Nevertheless, Andropov sent a three-page reply to Samantha, comparing her to Becky in *Uncle Tom's Cabin* and reassuring her that the Soviet Union was doing everything it could to avoid a nuclear world war and to stop making nuclear weapons. He also invited her to visit the USSR.

Andropov's reply caused a storm of controversy in the media. But Sam flew out to Moscow and toured the USSR, meeting children of her own age. She returned to Manchester a heroine. She wrote a book called *Journey to the Soviet Union*, "dedicated to the children of the whole world". She visited Japan and even starred in a Hollywood movie. But then, in August 1985, she lost her life in a fatal air crash. She was only thirteen years old.

In the years that followed, the Soviet Union issued a postage stamp featuring Sam. They went on to name a diamond, a flower, a mountain and a planet after her. The first Goodwill Games in Moscow were dedicated to her memory. In her hometown in Maine a statue was erected which shows Sam releasing a dove, while a bear, symbol of both the Soviet Union and Maine, clutches at her leg. In Maine, the first Monday in June of each year is designated as "Samantha Smith Day".

The Cold War is now over.

146. Presenting the good news every day

In May 1984, a serious earthquake hit the region of Lazio-Abruzzo in central Italy. There were many casualties, and 40,000 buildings were destroyed. In the aftermath, among those bringing supplies and helping to build provisional shelters was a 66-year-old Corsican-born Protestant evangelist by the name of Jean Stefanini. He made endless journeys to the site, sharing the gospel with victims.

During the previous three decades, Jean had done much to distribute the Bible and spread the gospel in France. He had gone from door to door in towns and villages, and exhibited at fairs, in marketplaces and at factory gates. He had purchased a large plot of land to welcome gypsies and share the word of Jesus with them. He had built an evangelical chapel in a suburb of Bordeaux. He had used a bus in which to start up a biblical library, while also running youth camps in his native Corsica.

But things had not always been this way for Jean Stefanini. In the early 1940s, as a violent and politically aggressive young man who had distanced himself from Christ, he was thrown into prison and condemned to death for a crime he had not committed. The day scheduled for his execution was his 25th birthday, 6th February 1943. The judges entered his cell where he was the oldest of four prisoners, but to his surprise another inmate was taken away and executed. With his hands and feet chained up, Jean accidentally knocked into his Bible, the only book authorised in the cells of those condemned to death. It fell open at this passage: "I have called you by your name and you are mine."

That day, instead of being shot, Jean learned that his death penalty had been changed to 20 years' hard labour. He began to read the Bible with two other prisoners. Very soon, with permission from the prison authorities, an increasing number of inmates assembled every day from mealtime until the resumption of hard labour. Before long, Jean was organising meetings that brought together hundreds of fellow inmates in the prisons where he had to serve out his sentence. Yvonne Lalande, his prison visitor, not only became a Christian but also agreed to become his wife. They were married in the prison. After ten years, Jean obtained a pardon.

> On my liberation, I immediately undertook to present the Good News of Jesus every day. I have done so ever since.

Even today, aged 85, Jean Stefanini, retired and living in Calvi in his native Corsica, is pastor of the Evangelical Protestant Church that he and his wife founded.

147. Intelligence = God

In the 1970s, Charles B Thaxton, a PhD in chemistry, was a post-doctoral fellow at Harvard University, studying the history of science. Thaxton had an inner conflict. His Christian belief was wrestling with his scientific training. "I had a Christian heart, but, as yet, a pagan mind."

Part of that training stated that Darwin's evolutionary theory had overturned God's creative participation. Nature had evolved. But then, in 1984, Thaxton co-authored a book on chemical evolution with two other scientists, Walter L Bradley and Roger L Olsen. It provoked a storm of controversy. Entitled *The Mystery of Life's Origin: Reassessing Current Theories*, it argues, among other things, that the DNA molecule, the basis for life, is a message: information coded in a double helix. And a message is normally created and sent by an intelligence.

With a groundswell of agreement from scientists and mathematicians worldwide, the Intelligent Design Movement was born.

Intelligence = God.

148. An African peasant king

During the 1970s and 1980s, bloody revolutions ripped apart the East African country of Uganda. Especially violent was the brutal dictator Idi Amin, who killed as many as 300,000 of his fellow citizens.

Festo Kivengere had been born in a beehive-shaped grass hut. Grandson of the last in a long line of kings of the Bahororo tribe, Festo grew up worshipping spirits and caring for his father's large herd of cattle in the surrounding lion country. When Festo was ten, an African missionary came to his village and built a mud-hut church. Festo learned quickly how to read and write and went away to higher education. But he finally left college an atheist.

Then there was a Christian revival in East Africa. Festo became a Christian. In time he became the Anglican Bishop of Kigezi.

Idi Amin's attempt to stamp out all the Christians in his country forced Bishop Festo and his wife to flee Uganda. In exile, he wrote a book entitled *I Love Idi Amin.*

On the cross Jesus pardoned those around him. As evil as Idi Amin was, how can I do less towards him?

When Amin was finally thrown out of the country, hatred remained among the people. Until he died of leukemia in 1988, Festo did much to help heal the wounds left by the war.

I find it more difficult to minister to those who are suffering from prosperity. With prosperity comes a kind of deadening façade that numbs sensitivities.

149. Executioner becomes pastor

Between 1974 and 1979, under the Khmer Rouge dictatorship of Pol Pot, his military leader Tak Mok organised the genocide of some 1 million people in Cambodia. As head of the notorious Tuol Sleng interrogation, torture and extermination centre, Hon Pin *aka* Duch meticulously directed the executions of more than 16,000 prisoners. Only seven inmates survived. When Vietnamese forces intervened in 1979, Duch fled abroad.

It was in a refugee camp that he became a Christian. In 1993, he was baptised by a Colombian priest. Duch went on to study theology at a Christian college in California, becoming pastor of the Golden West Cambodian Christian Church in Los Angeles.

In 1999, the Cambodian government arranged for Duch's arrest, and he was placed on trial for genocide, to testify against other Khmer Rouge war criminals. When warned about death threats, pastor Duch remarked:

They can have my body; Jesus has my soul.

150. Ashamed drug baron

By the early 1980s, Cuban-born Jorge Valdés had become one of the wealthiest and most ruthless of the Colombian drug lords. Having previously been caught and imprisoned, this was already his second empire. He was making over one million dollars a month moving 300 kg of "white powder". He had planes, helicopters, million-dollar horses and a ranch. But two of his associates had died, his addiction to pornography had led to a rocky third marriage, and he was making the lives of his three children miserable. One night, Valdés was sleeping with two call girls when his two-year-old daughter, Krystle, knocked on the bedroom door, crying for him. "How could I be so evil?" Jorge thought. He found his daughter whimpering on the hard floor. Stricken with shame, he ordered the women out and scalded himself in the shower attempting to wash the feelings away.

Leaving the Colombian drugs cartel, and with more time to spend on his ranch, he began to take karate lessons from Tim Brooks, a seventh-degree black belt. But, as well as karate, Brooks wanted to share his Christianity with Valdés. Although Valdés declared, "I do not believe in God: I *am* God!", Brooks quietly replied, "What I have to give you, you do not have enough money to buy." Three years later he gave his life to Jesus Christ.

Even though his past caught up with him and he was betrayed, Jorge freely confessed and voluntarily gave up every asset he owned. He emerged from a reduced prison sentence a changed man. Having gained a university PhD, he married a Christian woman and they moved to Atlanta. There he went out onto the streets to witness to drug addicts like those who had once been the victims of his immoral empire. And, so as to remain free from the lure of big business, Jorge Valdés and his wife now run a small carpet- and sewage-cleaning business.

151. Ballerina discovers Christ's love

When Mireille Nègre was two years old, her foot was badly crushed in an accident in a lift. Following seven operations and near-amputation, a doctor advised her parents that she should take up classical dance as a form of physiotherapy. From four years of age she took private lessons, but three years later she was attending the dance school of the Paris Opéra. In time she was given major parts in several of Tchaikovsky's famous ballets. At 21 years old, Mireille was regarded by impresario Serge Lifar as his star dancer.

By this time she had begun to read books about religion, particularly the gospels. She discovered the love of Christ. Retiring from ballet, she went into a Carmelite nunnery at Limoges. Impresario Lifar found it hard to accept that God had "stolen" his best pupil.

For ten years, Mireille gave up dancing, but always questioned whether this was really the will of the Lord. Suffering from triple scoliosis, she resumed dancing to regain her health, training for a gruelling six hours per day.

During the 1980s, the Vatican altered its attitude to the role of women in orders: they could stay in the world but still devote their life to Christ. In May 1986, Mireille was officially authenticated by Cardinal Lustiger at a ceremony in Notre Dame Cathedral in Paris. Since then she has not only danced for Christ, but has established a small dance school and is author of three books: *I Will Dance for You*, *A Life Between Heaven and Earth* and *Dancing on the Stars*.

152. The Alpha Course

Nicky Gumbel's mother was mayor of the fashionable London Borough of Kensington and Chelsea, and his father was a barrister. Neither was a churchgoer. Gumbel went to one of England's most exclusive public schools, Eton in the royal borough of Windsor, during which time he was an atheist. While studying law at Oxford University, he set about reading the New Testament with a view to proving it wrong. A day or two of that changed him. After ten years at the Bar, Nicky Gumbel was ordained in 1986.

That year, Reverend Gumbel was appointed curate of Holy Trinity, Brompton (HTB), near Knightsbridge, London. For the past nine years, this church had been running a low-key course called "Alpha". Nicky now took this course and rewrote it, aiming it at many non-believers and lapsed church-goers who considered Christianity to be "boring, untrue and irrelevant".

The revised Alpha course went into action in 1990. Within one year, four Alpha courses had drawn in 600 people. In 1993, Nicky and his team of several Old Etonians released the Alpha materials to churches throughout the UK first, and then to the rest of Europe and North America, until there were 13,000 Alpha courses worldwide, attended by an estimated 500,000 in 80 countries.

Nor were these confined to the Anglican Church. The 7,000 Alpha courses running in Britain, 2,000 in the US, 160 in Germany and 129 in Russia are offered by churches of denominations ranging from Catholic to Baptist. So far, 1.5 million people worldwide have taken the course, with another 250,000 currently enrolled.

One reason for this success is Alpha's slick marketing and hugely efficient business acumen, with an annual turnover of $8.3 million. A 100-member, full-time staff runs the project from offices in HTB's grounds, keeping tabs on Alpha websites, on courses held in most of Britain's prisons and more than half of its universities, and on the Alpha books, videos, audio tapes, newspaper, and the 50 international Alpha conferences for church leaders organised every year by HTB.

The other reason is a former atheist barrister's faith in God.

153. Accepting Yeshua as Messiah

Helen Shapiro was brought up in an Orthodox Jewish home in the east end of London.

> We went to Shul on High Holy days and I remember really loving Purim, Succot, and, of course, Pesach, as a child. We lit candles on Shabbat. My brother attended cheder and had a Bar Mitzvah. I was always aware of my Jewishness, and loved it.

At fourteen, Helen Shapiro became a pop star. Norrie Paramour, a top producer for EMI Records, signed her up, alongside Cliff Richard and The Shadows. During the early 1960s Helen Shapiro enjoyed great success with several hit singles and albums – at one point selling 40,000 copies daily of her song *Walking Back to Happiness* during a 19-week chart run. But then she gradually faded from the pop-music charts. In the years that followed, the Jewish pop star dabbled in Buddhism, spiritualism and psychic phenomena, but was never satisfied.

Then close friends passed her a book called *Betrayed*. It had been written by Stan Telchin, an American-Jewish business-man whose daughter had phoned him one day to tell him that she had accepted Jesus as her Messiah. After his initial shock he had set out to prove her wrong through the Scriptures, and ended up as a believer himself!

Helen Shapiro, in turn, accepted Yeshua (Jesus) as her Messiah as foretold in the Old Testament. On 26th August 1987, Helen became a Christian, which in turn helped her to give up chain-smoking. From 1989, Helen Shapiro's calendar has been heavily booked with giving gospel concerts around the world and recording new albums. Among these is a song recorded with another famous Christian, Cliff Richard.

154. The evangelist's daughter

During the 1950s Billy Graham, an evangelical Baptist from North Carolina, USA, conducted highly organised revivalist campaigns in the USA, the UK and later in South America and the former Soviet Union. During this time he was often away from home, and his children had to grow up with an absentee father.

At first, Anne, the second of the Graham children, was sheltered from the expectations and the scrutiny of the press. But, during her teenage years, Anne began to feel inferior and ill at ease with other people. She began to sense the expectations others had of "Billy Graham's daughter", and, feeling that her siblings were more gifted than she was, she felt pressurised into living up to a standard that others had set. She seemed the least likely to follow in her world-famous father's footsteps.

> I resolved that pressure when I decided to live my life to please God. I knew if I pleased God, not everyone would be pleased, but the people I cared most about such as my parents, siblings and grandparents would be pleased. It was a very freeing decision, one that I have adhered to to the present day.

Having married aged only 18, as a young mother she began to desire consistent Bible study. This soon led to her starting up a Bible study fellowship which was immediately attended by 500 people.

By 1988, Anne Graham Lotz had set up AnGeL Ministries and become the author of three award-winning books.

155. "Without Jesus Christ, I am nothing"

By 1987, Michael Chang was becoming known as a prodigy in the fiercely competitive sport of tennis. Aged only fifteen, he was the youngest player to win a main-draw match at the US Open and the youngest to reach the US Open Tour semi-final.

His grandparents had given Michael a Bible. One evening, with nothing else to do, he decided to take a good look at it. That evening changed his life. In 1989, on becoming the youngest male player (at just seventeen years old) to win the French Open, Michael publicly stated, "I thank the Lord Jesus Christ because without him, I am nothing."

During the next decade, whenever Michael Chang won or lost a championship, he never hesitated to pray and give thanks to the Lord, in full view of his adoring public and the media.

156. Prayer topples wall

In 1961 Germany had been split into two states, one capitalist and the other communist, with a heavily guarded wall running right through the city of Berlin to prevent Easterners from "defecting" to the West. During the following 30 years families remained divided, and anyone attempting to cross the Berlin Wall was shot. The least likely scenario for the demolition of this wall was that it might lie with the prayers of Protestant church communities. But so it was.

From 1980 onwards, Christian leaders in East Germany were leading Bible studies and discussion groups exploring the theme of peace. Two pastors coined the phrase "peace without weapons", associating it with an image based on the biblical idea of beating swords into ploughshares, and found that they had started a nationwide movement. In 1983, Pastor Christoph Wonneberger of the St Nikolai Church in Leipzig began opening the church at 5 pm every Monday for anyone and everyone to pray for peace, beginning with the beatitudes read together in unison: "Blessed are the peacemakers . . ." After the prayer service, they would then march with signs and placards, sometimes earning themselves a beating from the police and armed forces.

Opposition groups wishing to change East Germany from within grew up in the shelter of the churches, and protested against the authorities in power in East Berlin. In Leipzig, the peace prayers and Monday demonstrations drew more and more non-violent protesters, despite brutal police intervention. In 1989 numbers increased greatly, and other churches joined in. These peaceful gatherings formed the core around which the peaceful protest demonstrations grew. The "New Forum" was founded on 9th September, as a loose coalition of Christians and "Greens". Soon, large and peaceful demonstrations were being held every week. These protests grew from a couple of hundred to an estimated 500,000 people, and led to the resignation on 18th October of Erich Honecker, quickly followed by the opening of the Berlin Wall on 9th November.

157. Persecuted pastor

In 1986, a pastor by the name of Laszlo Tökés began to preach the gospel boldly in the small Hungarian Reformed church at Timişoara, a city in western Romania. He openly opposed the human-rights violations of Communist dictator Ceauşescu. Within two years, membership of Tökés' congregation had swelled to 5,000.

To crush this, the Securitate secret police stationed armed officers in front of the church every Sunday. They hired thugs to attack Pastor Tökés. They confiscated his ration book. In the end, he was to be banished to a small country parish. But when the police arrived in December 1989 to hustle him away, they were prevented from doing so by a wall of humans from every Christian denomination. This human wall remained for two nights, singing and praying by candlelight. Finally the police broke down the church door, beat up Tökés and hustled him away.

But the protest was now taken up in Bucharest city square, where the cry had changed to one for political freedom. Troops fired on the protesters, causing hundreds of casualties. But then the army joined the revolt. Within days, the nation had risen up and the bloody dictator Ceauşescu was toppled.

158. Home for the homeless

Between 1965 and 1980, Gérard Poirier had built up a flourishing Simca-Chrysler car dealership in Brittany, northern France. Then he suffered health problems. He sold up and moved to the south-west of France. Here he decided to set up an estate agency, renting out flats. One day he was approached by an elderly lady, Madame Roumagne, who wanted to sell him an old apartment block in the Bordeaux suburb of Floirac. She had intended to give it to her son, but disapproved of his decision to divorce her beloved daughter-in-law. Six months later, Gérard Poirier acquired the block.

As a Christian, he had always taken a special interest in the welfare of his personnel. With his wife, he now decided to turn the apartment block into a welcoming home for men of all ages who had fallen on hard times and often ended up on the street.

Since then, for the past thirteen years, the Poiriers, along with a couple of volunteers, have kept open house for a "family" of over 30 of the fringe elements of society, providing them with shelter, clothing and food.

Their organisation has no name. The building has no name. It is, however, very close to where I live. And it is just one of many hundreds of thousands of "homes" run by those who at first sight seem "the least likely".

159. The Akamosoa Project

The poor of Madagascar, a Pacific island off the coast of southern Africa, might have expected a French or a European priest to come to their aid. But Father Pedro Opeka, of Slovenian origin, had been born and raised in Argentina. "God gave me a talent to build" he said. Indeed Pedro was an apprentice in the building trade when he constructed his first home for a poor family in the Andes. Although he became a missionary priest in the Lazarist Order of St Vincent de Paul, this did not stop him from building other homes for the poor in Buenos Aires.

Father Pedro arrived in Madagascar in 1970, and it was not long before he had built the first school there, aged only 22. In November 1989, the Argentinian priest made an important decision to move outside Antananarivo to a wasteland of hills and rubbish-dump slums on the island's central plateau. It was there that he set up the Akamasoa ("good friend") project.

Father Pedro's approach was a practical one: build villages to rehabilitate those in extreme poverty, including their children. Families arriving must agree to three principles: children must go to school; everybody must work constructively; rules must be obeyed. There was to be no stealing, no adultery, no alcohol.

The Akamosoa Project now has some 19 villages, rehabilitating some 20,000 families, with over 9,000 children attending school. There are also workshops where the Malgaches can learn trades and skills, including agriculture.

> We had no plan. But if you come somewhere and you are in a situation with so much pain and so much that is bad, you haven't time to think. You just have to look after those people.

160. God changes hearts

In the USSR, one duty of the KGB officers had been to eradicate Christianity. But with General Secretary Gorbachev's perestroika and consequent glasnost (openness of information), things changed, and the most unlikely situations arose. Here are just two examples.

In Latvia, Pastor Joseph Bondarenko had spent nine years in a Soviet gulag. Once released, he began to hold evangelistic meetings in the local library, and thereafter a small group of believers who had accepted the gospel met in rented halls. In the autumn of 1988, in the city of Rostov on the Don River in southern Russia, a man approached Bondarenko and pleaded for forgiveness. The Pentecostal preacher did not understand what the man was talking about. Then the stranger reached into his pocket and pulled out his KGB identification: "I am the one who put you behind bars. Please forgive me!"

Pastor Sergei Timokin leads CCC Christ Church in St Petersburg, opposite the city's KGB headquarters. He was previously imprisoned there for two years for preaching the gospel. One day, a woman in the church asked Pastor Timokin to pray for her husband. She told him that her husband used to be a KGB officer in charge of the prison. She had become a Christian at Pastor Timokin's church some years before. Her husband had recently confided in her that he had been responsible for keeping the pastor in prison for so long. Her husband had been coming to church every month for the last four years to hear Pastor Timokin preach, but he now had a problem. He had become paranoid. So the woman had brought her husband to Christ Church that day so that the ex-prisoner could pray for his persecutor.

161. Forgiveness is not cheap

In 1990, Michael Apsley, a New Zealand-born Anglican priest who had been working for the African National Congress during the apartheid régime, was exiled to Harare in Zimbabwe. That April, Father Michael was opening a letter when it exploded. It was a bomb sent by the terrorist Civil Co-operation Bureau. Michael lost both his hands and an eye, not to mention other injuries.

At the same time, the (unbanned) ANC and the South African National Party government were initiating exploratory peace talks.

As a Christian, Father Michael realised that there was only one thing to do. After leaving hospital, he returned to Cape Town, where in July 1993 he founded the Institute for the Healing of Memories, now known as the Trauma Centre for Survivors of Violence and Torture.

"Within the work that I now do," Michael explains, "having no hands can almost be my greatest asset, as no-one can say to me, 'but you haven't suffered'."

When the three men who sent the letter-bomb had been identified and arrested, Father Michael, who had had to undergo major brain surgery as a result of his wounds, remarked, "Forgiveness is a package – it's not glib, it's not cheap, it's not easy. There is a lot of pain. Perpetrators should show their willingness to put right the wrongs they have committed. If those who had hurt me are prepared to do this, I would love to offer my forgiveness."

In addition to ongoing work with survivors of human-rights violations and political violence, the Trauma Centre currently works with survivors of sexual and domestic violence, and victims of criminal violence. Very recently, they have focused on children as an integral part of building a strong society.

162. Abandoning Islam, embracing Christianity

Mehdi Dibaj was born into a very wealthy Muslim family in Iran – the least likely situation for someone to become a Christian. But then in the 1950s in his teens, Dibaj became a Christian after reading a religious tract. Being a Christian was not easy. In 1979, he was imprisoned for 68 days for his beliefs.

Five years later, the Reverend Dibaj was imprisoned again for his continued refusal to return to Islam. He remained in prison for the next nine years, his "punishment" including solitary confinement, mock executions and regular beatings. In 1988, his wife divorced him and returned to being a Muslim after being threatened with death by stoning. Church and family members took custody of his four children, baptised Mary, Joseph, Jesus and Angel.

In December 1993, the Islamic Court in the city of Sari, the provincial capital of Mazaudaran, condemned Reverend Dibaj to death. He was charged with apostasy, in other words, abandoning Islam and embracing Christianity.

Bishop Haik Hovsepian-Mehr, an Armenian pastor, decided

to speak out and share the news of the Reverend Dibaj's sentence with the world. Among those who reacted were Amnesty International, the US government, the Vatican, the French government – and the world's mass media. The Reverend Dibaj was released in January 1994. No sooner free, he started travelling around Iran, encouraging fellow Christians. Then five months later he was abducted in mysterious circumstances and murdered. Some said it was a form of revenge provoked by the international publicity and response to his imprisonment.

Some years before, writing to his son from prison, Mehdi penned these words, "What a privilege to live for our Lord, and to die for him as well."

163. Prison miracle

In Lewes (Sussex, England) the Norman Castle served as the town's prison hundreds of years ago. Much later, in Victorian times, today's prison – a forbidding fortress of a place – was specially built. Its inmates have included murderers, rapists, drug-pushers and robbers.

Then, in 1993, an Anglican chaplain called David Powe arrived and began to share the gospel with them. A miracle happened. Within two years, an estimated 900 prisoners had become Christians, including some murderers. Converts included a man who'd tried to kill his wife with a hammer – she too became a Christian, after seeing the change in her husband's life. Even prison officers were touched by the dramatic events. One of them became a Christian after an inmate told him that they had been praying for him for six days. With emotion, the officer said, "My wife has been praying for me for 28 years." The chaplain's wife, Gillian Powe, wrote a book about this miracle, entitled, *The Cross Between Thieves*.

164. Touched by an Angel

A BA graduate from Williams College, Massachusetts, Martha Williamson began her career as a television script-writer for a musical and comedy series.

In 1993, Martha was asked by CBS (Columbian Broad-casting System) television to produce a new one-hour drama series of secular entertainment. But Martha Williamson is a strong Christian. Having prayed to God, she arrived and told executives exactly how the show would "create a place every Sunday night where God is honored". The name of this ground-breaking series was *Touched by an Angel*. After two successful years, a second hour-long series was added, called *Promised Land*. At the time of writing, almost 900 episodes of *Touched by an Angel* have been broadcast. And Martha has received a string of awards for her Christian achievement.

165. Teacher in the backwoods

In 1912 a young schoolteacher was attempting to teach the impoverished schoolchildren in the backwoods of the Great Smoky Mountains in Tennessee. The folk in that area of Appalachia were wild, and the teacher found it an uphill struggle, but she persisted.

Many years later, the schoolteacher's daughter, Catherine Marshall, decided to write a book based on her mother's ex-periences. It tells of how a 19-year-old girl by the name of Christy Huddleston left a comfortable, sheltered home in North Carolina to teach in a school in Cutter Gap, Tennessee and how she came to care for the wild mountain people, guided by Miss Alice Henderson, and make a difference in their lives. The 500-page novel, called *Christy*, was published in 1967. To date it has sold 8 million copies and been read by 35 million people.

Among those who read it was the son of a Christian minister and Sunday-school teacher by the name of Ken Wales, who had become an actor, then director, then producer in Hollywood. For 20 years, Wales campaigned to obtain the rights to make *Christy* into a TV series. His prayers were answered. The CBS production of *Christy* attracted a staggering 44 million viewers to its première on Easter Sunday 1994.

It is very unlikely that those backwoods children in 1912 ever dreamed that their teacher would become so well known . . .

166. A timid teenage singer

Amy Grant has sold nearly 18 million records worldwide, won five grammy awards, 17 Dove awards including "Artist of the Year" four times and has performed everywhere from the White House to The Grand Ole Opry to Monday Night Football.

In 1991 her album *Heart in Motion* was certified quadruple platinum, signifying sales of over four million copies. The project spent 52 weeks on Billboard's Top 200 album chart, spawning four Top Five hits including "Baby, Baby", which topped both the Billboard and the rock and roll charts simultaneously. The success of *Heart in Motion* took Amy's career to an even higher level and generated tremendous exposure, including over a dozen appearances on the major American TV shows.

Amy Grant has taken Christian music and the Christian message to a wider audience and a broader platform than any other artist in the contemporary Christian genre.

And yet, when she released her self-titled début album at the age of fifteen, Amy was so nervous in the recording studio that she insisted on singing with the lights off.

Amy doesn't limit her encouragement and support of others strictly to her musical endeavours. She participates in Nashville's Leadership Music Program and meets with terminally ill children as part of the "Make-a-Wish" Foundation. She recently played right field in Nashville's City of Hope Celebrity Softball Challenge, and has shown her skills on the green by participating in celebrity golf tournaments to aid various causes. She has hosted benefits for the American Cancer Society, the American Heart Association and the Nashville Symphony.

167. Chinese quadriplegic surgeon finds comfort through Joni's story

While Dr Zhang Xu, a 34-year-old orthopaedic surgeon from Anshan, China, was on holiday in the Yemen, he broke his neck in a bizarre diving accident. He became a quadriplegic for life. At first no-one would help him commit suicide.

Then, in 1997, a Japanese physiotherapist sent Zhang Xu a tattered copy of *Joni* (see story 124 on page 119). Xu's mother read this to him as he lay immobile in his lonely bed.

Not only did he discover the love of Christ, but before long, helped by his mother and using an old American-Chinese dictionary, he translated *Joni* into Chinese. With Joni Eareckson Tada's blessing, the government-owned Huaxia Publishing Company brought out the book.

In October 2001, when Joni visited Beijing, she met Zhang Xu and together they were wheeled onto the Great Wall.

168. France's most popular sportsman

Judo: becoming a *judoka* might not appear to be compatible with being a Christian. Can forceful wrestling sit alongside gentle caring?

Frenchman David Douillet has achieved a mercurial success in this sport of Japanese champions that is more wedded to the Shinto religion. From being French champion in 1991, he was four times world champion, as well as gold medallist in the Olympic Games, first in Atlanta and then in Sydney. He is therefore the most titled *judoka* in the history of the sport.

But David is also a practising Christian: "I have become a believer. I was aiming at being a non-practising Catholic, but I have become a Protestant. Faith is simple: you just need to believe. I talk to him. I never ask for victory, but just to give the best of myself and not be injured."

Voted France's most popular sportsman in 2000, David has used his celebrity status to gain money for charitable causes. This has included a much publicised annual event "TGV – *pièces jaunes*", where he joined Bernadette, the wife of France's President Chirac, on a train journey to collect "small change" money to build a new children's hospital in Paris.

169. All things are possible . . .

In the early 1990s, Kurt Warner was an unknown footballer, freshly graduated from North Iowa University, USA, and working at a local supermarket for $5.50 per hour. Around this time, Kurt and his wife, Brenda, became Christians, learning that with faith everything is possible. At the end of the 1997 season, Kurt Warner signed on with the St Louis Rams as a quarterback. With his life and faith woven together, Kurt went from being a National Football League bench-warmer (reserve player) to becoming the League's "Most Valued Player" within six months.

In 1999, he led the Rams to their first Super Bowl victory, and became one of the great NFL players of all time. He completed 325 of 499 passes for 4,353 yards. His 65% completion rate was remarkable; plus he threw for 41 touchdowns while being intercepted thirteen times. His passer rating of 109.2 is the fifth highest single season total in NFL history. In one match, he threw the ball a record 414 yards.

With a phenomenal following, Kurt has created his own trading card that he autographs for fans. The front of the card shows the 6'2", 220-lb quarterback getting ready to pass the pigskin. It also contains the New Testament passage: "All things are possible through Christ who strengthens me" (Philippians 4:13). On the back of the card is Warner's testimony – and a prayer.

Out of his winnings, Kurt donated $200,000 to Camp Barnabas, a Christian summer camp for children with disabilities.

170. Boy speaks for AIDS victims

According to the United Nations, at the start of the 21st century around 25.3 million people in sub-Saharan Africa were infected with HIV/AIDS. Some 4.2 million of these lived in South Africa. About 13 million African children had lost their parents through HIV/AIDS. And yet South African President Thabo Mbeki did not at first see the necessity to react.

But then Nkosi Johnson spoke up. This little boy had been orphaned at only two years old. He was adopted by a kindly lady called Gail Johnson and grew up in her home in Johannesburg. When told that he could not attend school because of his incurable illness, Nkosi and Gail took their case to the national parliament. This resulted in new legislation forbidding discrimination against people with the deadly virus.

Nkosi became a national figure, and from then on began to give speeches around South Africa, urging people to practise safe sex. By the time he died, aged only twelve, in June 2001, Nkosi Johnson had become an international symbol of AIDS Concern. One thousand mourners attended his funeral at the Methodist church and hymns were sung in English, Zulu and Xhosa.

His adoptive mother, Gail, said of him, "Nkosi gave me unconditional love and acceptance."

171. Haven for Ground Zero workers

The Reverend Daniel Paul Matthews was rector of the Episcopalian Trinity Church, with its 235-year-old chapel of St Paul. He was coming up to retirement. The two towers of the World Trade Center, symbols of the tough world of banking and commerce, stood proudly 150 yards from his church door. Indeed he was there when, on 11th September 2001, two terrorist-hijacked commercial airliners were deliberately crashed into those towers. Although 2,819 people lost their lives in the destruction that followed, Trinity Church was untouched, except for ashes in its garden.

In the weeks that followed, the gentrified city church suddenly found itself the only calm spot in a war zone. Reverend Matthews admitted, "There isn't anything we trained to do for this." And yet it became a haven for Ground Zero workers, providing spiritual solace and physical healing, grief counselling and tables full of donated food, blankets and boots.

Alongside this, many business-minded people who managed to survive the attack became good Samaritans and indeed caring Christians thereafter.

172. United in crisis

In April 2002, Israeli tanks moved into Bethlehem as part of a series of raids on West Bank cities. Local civilians and Palestinian militants alike sought refuge in churches throughout the city. They moved into Manger Square, believing that Israeli troops would not fire on them. The Israeli forces fired into the square. About 200 people, including Palestinian gunmen, nuns, priests and civilians, took refuge inside the Church of the Nativity, meant to mark the spot where Jesus was born.

The custodian of this church was a black-haired, bespectacled, 38-year-old Franciscan by the name of Ibrahim Faltas, born and educated in Cairo. He was used to organising Christmas-time celebrations.

"I had never found myself in a crisis before and I decided to take responsibility, co-operating with all the people around me to end it peacefully."

By praying every day, Father Ibrahim shepherded his unusual flock through a 39-day siege of the Church of the Nativity, warding off hunger and tension while dodging gunfire from Israeli troops outside and Palestinians inside.

The siege finally ended with a deal worked out following intervention by the Vatican, the European Union and the United States. Thirteen of the gunmen were exiled to Cyprus, 26 others were taken to the Gaza Strip, and the rest were released.

Looking back, Faltas was able to point to a positive aspect

of the tense stand-off. The ancient church is divided into fief-doms ruled by often competing Christian denominations. Disputes over schedules and sites have turned violent in the past. For now at least, that is all over. "We were all living together wonderfully. We became brothers united in this crisis," he said. "I hope there will be peace between the two peoples, Palestinians and Israelis," Father Ibrahim told the world press.

*   *   *

As these brief sketches illustrate, the grace of God is contained in jars of clay: men and women whose faithfulness allowed God to use them, whatever their limitations. I find this a true message of hope, and a source of joy. May the Lord show you the part you can play in his purposes.

Maybe you are one of his least likely?

FOR FURTHER READING . . .

Augustine, Saint, Bishop of Hippo *Confessions*, New York: Doubleday, 1960

Bright, Bill *Five Steps to Christian Growth*, Orlando, Florida: New Life Publications, 1994

Brother Andrew *God's Smuggler*, New American Library, 1987

Bunyan, John *The Pilgrim's Progress*, Oxford: OUP, 1984

Burgess, Alan *Small Woman*, Servant Publications, 1985

Chesterton, GK *Saint Francis of Assisi*, New York: Image Books, 1987

Colson, Charles *Born Again*, Boston, MA: GK Hall & Co., 1976

Douglas, Lloyd C *The Magnificent Obsession*, New York: Pocket Books, 1943

Douglas, Lloyd C *The Robe*, Boston, Mass: Houghton Mifflin Co., 1942

Eareckson, Joni *Joni*, Grand Rapids, MI: Zondervan, 1980, 2001

Graham, Franklin and Lockerbie, Jeanette *Bob Pierce: This One Thing I Do*, Nashville, TN: Thomas Nelson, 1983

Guinness, Alec *Blessings in Disguise*, London: Fontana, 1985

Joad, Cyril EM *Recovery of Belief*, London: Faber and Faber, 1953

Kerr, Pat and Hill, Susan *Down to Earth*, London: Ebury Press, 1992

King, Martin Luther, Jr *Strength to Love*, New York: Harper & Row, 1963

Kivengere, Festo *I love Idi Amin,* Old Tappan, NJ: Spire Books, 1977

Lewis, CS *Surprised by Joy*, London: Geoffrey Bles, 1956

Marshall, Catherine *Christy*, New York: McGraw Hill, 1967

Morison, Frank *Who Moved the Stone?*, London: Faber and Faber, 1930

Mother Teresa *My Life for the Poor*, London: Harper Collins, 1985

Muggeridge, Malcolm *Jesus Rediscovered*, New York: Doubleday, 1969

Nègre, Mireille *I Will Dance for You*, Paris: Desclee de Brouwer, 1XXX

Pascal, Blaise *Pensées*, London: Everyman's Library, 1973 (1660)

Pullinger, Jackie *Chasing the Dragon*, London: Hodder & Stoughton, 1980

Smith, Samantha *A Journey for Peace*, Boston: Minneapolis Dillon Press, 1987

Stowe, Harriet Beecher *Uncle Tom's Cabin*, Cambridge, MA: Harvard Library Classics, 1962

Telchin, Stan *Betrayed!*, London: Marshall Pickering, 1981

Ten Boom, Corrie *The Hiding Place*, Grand Rapids, MI: Chosen Books, 1971

Ten Boom, Corrie and Buckingham, Jamie *Tramp for the Lord*, Grand Rapids, MI: Fleming H Revell, 1998

Thaxton, Charles *The Mystery of Life's Origin*, Dallas, Texas: Lewis and Stanley Foundation for Thought and Ethics, 1984

Jorge Valdés, Ken Abraham, *Coming Clean*, Waterbrook Press, 1999

Varah, Chad *Before I Die Again*, London: Constable and Co. Ltd, 1992

Wallace, Lew *Ben-Hur*, New York: Harper, 1880

Wilkerson, David *The Cross and the Switchblade*, New York: Pyramid Books, 1962

Wurmbrand, Richard *Tortured for Christ*, Bartlesville, OK: Living Sacrifice Book Co., 1998 (Mainz: Matthiou Grunewald, 1967)

Using Internet search engines may provide a great deal more information about the least likely people mentioned in this little book . . . and indeed about those not mentioned!

ALPHABETICAL INDEX

Numbers after entries refer to pages.